KEEPING THE FAITH

CHURCH OF ROME OR CHURCH OF CHRIST?

Tony Flannery

MERCIER PRESS

Mercier Press
Douglas Village, Cork
Email: books@mercierpress.ie
Website: www.mercierpress.ie

Trade enquiries to CMD Distribution
55A Spruce Avenue, Stillorgan Industrial Park
Blackrock, County Dublin
Tel: (01) 294 2560; Fax: (01) 294 2564
E-mail: cmd@columba.ie

ISBN 1 85635 484 9
10 9 8 7 6 5 4 3 2 1

A CIP record for this title is available
from the British Library

Mercier Press receives financial assistance from
the Arts Council/An Chomhairle Ealaíon

Printed and Bound by J. H. Haynes & Co. Ltd, Sparkford

CONTENTS

PREFACE

I dreamt last night that I was back in the seminary. I was facing some sort of final exam. As is often the case with dreams, it wasn't clear exactly which exam I was preparing for, but it was going to be significant if I was to continue in my chosen profession. I understand that many people have a recurring dream. For a long period of my life I have regularly dreamed that I am within a few days of my final second-level exam for which I have not done the required work. I experience a sense of urgency that I must get down to work and study hard for the last few days, but another part of me is saying not to worry, that I will get through it none the less. I read somewhere that this is the most common of all recurring dreams. I suspect psychologists would tell me that it portrays some innate anxiety or insecurity in my personality, possibly dating from childhood. In recent years that dream has become less frequent, and I cannot quite remember the last occasion I had it. So when it came again last night I could feel myself almost welcoming it like an old friend I hadn't seen for a long while. This time, however, the dream was different. It was located in the seminary and, instead of studying for the impending exams, I decided I would not sit them at all and that I would find a new direction for my life. Mostly I do not remember dreams very clearly, but this morning I had a distinct memory of a sense of relief at a decision well made. That tells something about my present relationship with the church as I come towards the end of the sixth decade of my life. And that is partly why I am writing this book about the Catholic church. It is not a book about myself, but I need to give the context out of which the book is coming. In my real life I didn't make the decision to leave the seminary and find a new direction. Instead I went on to ordination, though not without many questions, and I have lived and worked the last thirty-one years of my life as a priest, and member of a religious community, in Ireland. I have been, and continue to be, a populist preacher, conducting missions and novenas. In many ways they have been good years. It was a type of work that suited my particular talent and personality, and I have enjoyed it. But the questions have remained, maybe no longer the ones I began with but others that knowledge about life and how the church operates have raised for me. I think I have changed a great deal, both in what I believe and what I no longer find tenable.

In my early years as a priest I spent many hours in confession boxes, working my way through long lines of penitents. I can often remember peeping out through the slit in the curtain to see if there was any sign of the queue of people coming to an end. The queues were long because in our preaching we emphasised the importance of going to confession during the mission or novena event that we were conducting. The people would not have participated properly in the event, we told them, unless they went to confession. It was an era in which we were making a big effort to improve the quality of confession as we understood it. So we urged people to do an inventory of their lives rather than reciting a simple list of sins which was the common practice at the time. I tended to regard the quality of the confessions I heard as an indicator of how the mission was going, and also an indicator of whether our preaching was getting through to the people. I was young and energetic, so long hours in the confession box were not a problem; in fact hearing people's confessions made me feel good. I got a sense that I was making a contribution to their lives, and while I had some doubts, particularly in relation to scrupulous people, I believed I was generally doing good work.

I now question the usefulness of that form of confession, except as a very occasional event in a person's life. I hardly ever go into a confession box anymore in my role as confessor, and never as penitent. Instead I promote the celebration of the communal forms of reconciliation, pushing out as much as possible the boundaries of what the church authorities allow, and going as close to giving general absolution as we dare in the particular circumstances. I am no longer interested in urging people to do an inventory of their lives in confession, or to give me a long recitation of their sins. I have come to believe that the sacrament is more about God and his attitude towards us than about the particular state of the penitent's life. If a person has an awareness of their need for forgiveness, and if they wish, however feebly, to try to change and live out the values of Jesus more fully, then I am happy to speak the words of absolution over them without needing to hear any more. If there is a person who wishes to talk about some aspect of their life, of course I will sit and listen, and give whatever meagre advice I can, but I prefer to keep that separate from the sacrament, and I do not put any pressure on people to come for this type of encounter. I believe that it is only occasionally in a person's life that they may need to do an inventory of their lives, or discuss a particular problem, and the choice of when and to whom they do it must be left completely to the person themselves. I have known some priests down through the years who seemed to me to exercise the ministry of confession in order to meet their own needs rather than that of the penitents, their need to feel that what they were doing was significant, to exercise control over people's mind and lives and, in occasional instances, to feed their own frustrations or fantasies.

In my younger days I had the temerity to preach a great deal about marriage. It was one of the standard topics on a week of mission or novena. I proclaimed the ideal of Christian marriage as a lifelong commitment of love between a man and a woman. I even had the nerve to talk about the problems of marriage and how they could be overcome. I believed that the fact that I was not married myself did not disqualify me from addressing the topic. I am much less sure now, both of what needs to be said, and of my competence to say it. In any given congregation today there will be people in many other forms of relationship besides the lifelong committed relationship between a man and a woman which the church understands as marriage. There will be people in second relationships, maybe more secure and happy in them than in earlier marriages which they entered into before they were mature enough to understand. There will be single parents, and people who were brought up by one parent and who have never experienced the type of family life that we regard as normal. And there will of course be gay people, maybe in relationships. Meeting so many people over the years has made me less sure about my earlier certainties. Studying the history and development of Christian marriage added to my questions. For instance, Michael G. Lawler in his book *Secular Marriage, Christian Sacrament*, highlights three of the developments that I wondered about:

> First, a very negative attitude towards sexuality and its use in marriage crept into Christianity from heretical Gnostic and Stoic sources. Though this attitude was combated consistently by theologians and church councils, it remains still rooted in the ongoing Christian ethos about marriage. Secondly, this negative attitude towards sexuality contributed to the enthronement, however implicit, of several judgements in the Catholic tradition. Among these are: marriage, involving sexuality and therefore somehow evil, cannot be a cause of grace, that is, cannot be a sacrament; virginity and celibacy are superior, and therefore preferable, to marriage; Holy Orders and those in Holy Orders are holier, and therefore superior, to marriage and those in marriage. These judgements have left their mark on the Roman Catholic tradition; they are quite nonsensical when measured against the biblical tradition. Finally, with the acceptance of Christian marriage as a sacrament, came the need to specify just when a sacramental marriage took place and was indissoluble.

This last point opened up a can of worms for the church, which led to the development of the annulment courts. I believe it was a mistake for the church to ever get involved in this aspect of marriage regulation. I have seen something of the workings of the annulment courts, and how they vary from one country to another, and even from one region to another. And yet their decision carries enormous consequences for the believer. The person who is judged worthy of an annulment can happily enter into another marriage with the blessing of the church, and continue to be a full member of the church, receiving the sacraments. The person who is rejected is faced with living a single life, or else entering into a relationship not sanctioned by the church, and being deprived of the sacramental life; some even suggest that they will be deprived of salvation, since they are judged to be living in a state of serious sin. This judgement is made in a legalistic way, and without reference to the degree of love or commitment that may be present in a second relationship in that person's life. Being involved in the legalities of marriage is a minefield for the church.

At one time I regarded myself as being able to preach good sermons on sexuality. I was not going to adhere to the style of traditional sermons preached on the topic when I was growing up. These laid down incredibly strict laws on sexual behaviour and imposed them under pain of mortal sin and eternal damnation. I tried to adopt what I considered a more enlightened approach for our time. I set out to explain the church's teaching, and show that it was the reasonable and sensible option, the common sense way to live, and that living in this way would lead to happiness in this life, and also in the next. I was trying to counter the perceived notion that everything the church had to say on this topic began with the word 'no'. I used to argue that a sexual relationship that did not occur in the context of a long-term and publicly committed relationship was not really meaningful, because this was the fundamental meaning of the act of intercourse. It was a well worked-out talk, and seemed to me to be convincing in its logicality. One evening, after this talk, a young married woman challenged my position. She said that while what I had said sounded reasonable, it was not a valid or healthy attitude for the world in which we live. She pointed out that most women today do not marry until they are in their late twenties. 'Do you expect them,' she said, 'to abstain from sex until that age? What are they to do with all the enormous sexual energy of their twenties? Are you telling me that bottling all that up, and not giving expression to it, is a healthy thing to do? It would lead to frustration and neurosis.' I didn't fully agree with her and am not sure that I now do, but she forced me to look again at what I was saying, and to recognise that passion, desire, energy, longing and love were all part of this question, and that they could not be easily captured in a well-reasoned, but detached, talk. As I began to study the topic more closely, and come to know some of the unfortunate influences at work in the development of church teaching on sex and on marriage, I found that I increasingly left the subject out of my schedule of sermons.

In my first year as a mission preacher I was sitting one day with a more senior colleague as we worked out our topics for the week's preaching. He immediately announced that we would have a sermon on Our Lady. When I demurred, having a great many other topics that I thought should be dealt with, he told me that as a Redemptorist I should never preach at any event, long or short, without giving a talk on Our Lady. I continued to do so for years. I preached about Mary as the woman of faith, Mary as the virgin most pure, the Holy Family as the perfect example of family life, and many others.

But now I have many questions about the use the church has made of Our Lady down through the centuries, and how issues like her virginity and her submissiveness, probably based on ancient myths rather than historical reality, have shaped attitudes and teaching about women and marriage, and have been used to oppress people, and restrict their freedom. Recent developments around reported apparitions and messages of Our Lady have been even more disturbing, and I can see how particular shrines and reputed apparitions have been used in a very political way by people who have particular traditionalist agendas within the church. Of all the topics I deal with in this book, this one is probably the most difficult, because devotion to Our Lady is very emotionally charged in Catholic life. Yet, as I explain later, I see the need for significant reform here.

In the past I have preached about vocations to the priesthood and religious life, and have urged young men to consider if they might have a vocation to the priesthood. I even, for a very short period of time, was appointed as the official promoter of vocations for my congregation. I don't ask anyone to become a priest or to enter religious life any more. I am a member of a religious community which has gone through a major decline in my lifetime. I am now convinced it is in a terminal condition, and that we are so old and tired that we are no longer entitled to invite young men to join us. I have come to the very difficult conclusion that we are dying out, and that the only option open to us is to try to do so as gracefully as we can. I do not believe that religious life as such will disappear. It has always been a feature of the church and will continue to be so. The particular form of religious life that has blossomed over the past 200 years, apostolic religious life, does seem to me to have served its time. I do not believe that new forms will grow out of the embers of what we have been. Instead I believe that we must die out in order to make space for the new to grow. And, as is the way with the Spirit of God, what is new will grow from unlikely sources, and will take forms that will be unexpected and different.

As regards priesthood, I have come to know the damage that

the structure and culture of clericalism has caused. I am convinced that the present form of priesthood is one of the main bulwarks of the power structure that is oppressing the church. The office of priesthood needs to be opened up to married people and to women. But that is not the whole, or even a significant part of the answer to the problem. Ministry in the Catholic church needs to be radically redefined, as I outline later in this book. By encouraging young men into the present system of priesthood I believe I would be only sustaining a system that is in urgent need of reform.

I used to preach about the importance of going to mass every Sunday, and how this was essential for the preservation of the faith. I still believe that the community dimension of our faith is at the core of what it is about, and I also believe that the Eucharist is the life-blood of Christian community. But I know that what happens in many of our churches on a Saturday evening or Sunday morning does little justice either to the Eucharist or the Christian community. Our masses are often devoid of both prayerfulness and celebration. The Vatican authorities in recent times seem to be so concerned about the proper rubrics, restoring old Latin formulations in new translations of the mass texts, and keeping the laity in their place, that they are restricting rather than helping the necessary reforms. Many of our parishes, particularly in large towns and cities, have in reality no community, and the large churches do not bring people together in any sense other than the physical. We need to find new structures for our Eucharist. These will be built around smaller groups with a real sense of belonging. The leader of the community, meaning the priest, should be chosen from among the community. The Eucharist should never be used as a moral weapon, as some Catholics are doing today by suggesting that people should be refused communion because of their political views or their lifestyle. There must be a welcome for everyone who genuinely wishes to be there and to participate, whatever the circumstances of their lives or the frequency of their attendance. There must be great freedom allowed to each individual to work out their own personal relationship with God. The church is there as a guide and a help, not a dictator.

All of the above makes it clear that I am critical of many aspects of the church as it exists today. While I have no doubt that the Spirit of God was at work in the beginning, and continues to be present in the church, I have come to the conclusion that the present Catholic church cannot claim divine origin for every aspect of its structure and its interpretation of the teaching of Christ. This has been the biggest change that I have experienced. It has meant that I now question official statements from the Vatican, rather than seeing them as the voice of God for myself and all church members. Equally it has meant that I no longer accept that the church is the repository of all truth, but that truth can be discovered in many places, people and beliefs. I believe that the church's core message is true but it does not have the monopoly on truth. I know that I am not alone, or even particularly unusual in this personal journey that I have outlined above. Many other priests, and indeed lay people, have gone through the same changes of belief and attitude – but not all. Many times I have been told by certain members of the church that I should do the honest thing, and leave the church. Some of my contemporaries have done so. But I have chosen to stay, and to work for the sort of changes that I see as essential to the survival of the church, or at least its survival as an appropriate vehicle of the message of Christ. Thankfully I have not lost the faith. In some ways it is deeper than ever before.

What do I preach now? I am less moralistic and more biblical than I used to be. As a consequence I have to work harder to retain an effective level of communication. In the past I would have preached for half an hour or more at the evening mission

service, giving great emphasis to the living of a moral life. Now I
try to involve people in the presentation of the message, using
music, drama, dance wherever possible. It is a very different style
of mission. I have come to the conclusion that preaching about
commandments, laws and teachings is a futile exercise unless the
listener has been attracted to the source of these teachings, Jesus
Christ. Only when a person has come to know Christ will all the
rest begin to make sense. We can no longer presume faith in our
listeners, even those who attend church. So we must give much
more attention to the basics than we did in the past. This is more
difficult in terms of preaching. It is harder to hold the attention
of a congregation when you are talking about some aspect of the
life of Jesus as presented in the Gospels than if you were launch-
ing an attack on, for instance, corrupt business practices or fornication. That is why I try to use a variety of methods of communication. I believe that our faith is first and foremost faith in a
person. I preach most of all about the love of God for humanity.

A friend recently lamented the absence of fear in my preaching. He recalled the old-style preaching, and how it was so much
more effective in keeping people on what he called 'the straight
and narrow'. I can see the truth in what he was saying. Fear is certainly a way of keeping people under control. But I have learned
to listen to the words of St John's Gospel: 'Perfect love drives out
fear.' People should come to Jesus because they are attracted to
him, drawn by the wonder of his person and his message, and respond to him in love. That is why I struggle to communicate Jesus,
rather than laws and commandments. I tell the Gospel stories
again, trying to paint a picture of what he was like, how he re-
lated to people. I have put a lot of work into doing dramatic pre-
sentations of some of the great Gospel stories. I try to highlight
what an exciting and radical person he was, in his lifestyle, his
attitudes and his teaching. When I talk about the church I present it as the community of the followers of Jesus, the custodian of

the stories, and the people who are struggling to give a witness to what he stood for: 'by this shall everyone know that you are my disciples, if you love one another.'

I am more convinced than ever that the Christian message is powerful, and that it has an answer to the deepest problems besetting humanity today, if only we could put it into practice. That is what sustains me, and keeps me active in the ministry despite all the change that has happened in my life and views over the past thirty years, and my increasing unhappiness with the current state of things in the Catholic church.

This is the context out of which this book comes. Because of where I have lived and worked its focus is very much on the church in what we would call the western or the developed world, if it is possible to use any of those descriptions nowadays without sounding patronising. My aim in my preaching and writing has always been to communicate complex and difficult ideas about life and faith in a way that will make sense to the average person who has not studied theology or scripture. This is what this book is trying to do.

I

THE WORD OF GOD AND TRADITION

It is no secret to anybody that the Catholic church is going through a time of crisis, particularly in the western world. Numbers attending church are falling in most countries in the west, vocations to the priesthood are in sharp decline, and the revelations of sexual abuse by priests and religious have been shocking and deeply damaging. In this book I will try to explain the major issues facing the church as I see them, giving some idea of where the problems originated, and hopefully providing some guidance on how to deal with them. I will give an historical background to each of the issues, because that is crucial in understanding the present difficulties. As Catholics we belong to a church that has a long history. It cherishes its history, and it is right to do so. But a balance needs to be found between the past and the present, and it seems to me that there is a strong inclination in the church to live in the past, and to treat whatever is new and modern with suspicion. It has honoured and revered the great men (and a few women) of the past, and preserved their teaching, but it often treats with suspicion and distrust the great people in the church today.

The Catholic church teaches that the Word of God, the source of all that we believe, is found in two places, the Bible and what it calls tradition. These two are equally important sources for learning about God's relationship with humanity and what his will is for us. Finding the true Word of God both in the Bible and in tradition is not as simple as might appear. The Bible is a difficult and complex book, written by numerous different people over a period of maybe 2,000 years. Some Christian churches, particularly those known as evangelical, believe that every word and sentence in the Bible is divinely inspired, means exactly what it says and must be taken literally. They do not allow for any interpretation, based on the difficulty of understanding the language or the culture of the time in which it was written, or for any other reason. What is on the page, in the language in which they are reading it, is the Word of God for them. That is a difficult position to sustain, unless very selective texts of the Bible are examined. There are some strange passages in the Old Testament particularly which, if interpreted literally, would have us doing things that don't make much sense, and in some cases are decidedly un-Christian. For instance, chapter fourteen of the book of Deuteronomy tells us not to eat pigs' meat because they do not chew the cud. In chapter seventeen we are told that if we know anyone who is worshipping an idol or a false god we are to take them out of the town and stone them to death. The book of Leviticus gives some interesting instruction which in my role as a priest I am glad people are not taking literally. In chapter fourteen it says: 'Anyone who finds mildew in his house must go and tell the priest about it. The priest shall order everything to be moved out of the house before he goes to examine the mildew.' I don't remember my seminary training covering that particular aspect of priestly ministry!

Because there is so much that is culturally conditioned in the book, the Catholic church holds that the Bible needs interpretation. But this attitude to our sacred book is not without difficulty either. The problem arises when new Bible scholarship discovers things that are different from, or even contrary to, what was generally believed and taught by the great scholars of the past. This has happened a lot in recent years. After long centuries of stagnation in Catholic Bible scholarship, the last fifty years have seen great developments in this area, and an enormous growth in knowledge and understanding of the Bible. These have been helped by the discovery of ancient documents, and new insights into the culture and language of the time of Jesus. Many interesting and quite significant issues have been raised, for example the type of church, if any, Jesus intended to set up; the development of ministry in the early church' and the story of the origin and birth of Jesus. These need to be re-examined, and I will attempt to deal with them in this book. While the Catholic church is a long way ahead of some other Christian denominations in its understanding of the Bible, it is still fair to say that it has shown itself to be uncomfortable with new knowledge, and has often experienced great difficulty in relinquishing beliefs that have come down through the centuries.

Our emphasis on the importance of tradition is one of the major things that differentiates Catholic teaching from that of the other Christian churches. But interpreting tradition is no less complex than interpreting the Bible. By tradition the church means the wealth of knowledge and understanding of our faith that has come down to us from the great teachers and writers in the church. People like Saints Augustine, Bonaventure and Thomas Aquinas have left behind volumes of writing that have shaped many of our current dogmas and beliefs. They have contributed hugely to Catholic tradition. But is tradition, as we understand it, a static or an active thing? In other words, is tradition something that has been handed down to us from previous generations as a body of unchanging and unchangeable knowledge and dogma? Or is tradition something fluid, something that is constantly changing and developing as new knowledge and new insights from the great minds of today are added to the mix? In this, as in other areas, the church is more comfortable holding on to historical tradition than trying to integrate modern ideas into its belief and practice. For instance, in the last one hundred years or so we have come to a new understanding of human reproduction, indeed of human sexuality generally, and while theology has taken this on board, church teaching has been much more reluctant to do so, with serious consequences which I will deal with in a later chapter. Equally, when democracy and the equality of men and women began to be more widely accepted in society generally, the church dug in its heels for centuries, and refused to accept them. They did this because, even though these ideas are in harmony with central teachings of Christ, they contradicted many of the assumptions of the past, assumptions on which certain church teachings were based. This slowness of the church to integrate new knowledge is becoming an increasing problem as the general rate of change accelerates. It is being more and more left behind. Can the church learn how to change quickly enough to integrate the new knowledge? Can it, as the Second Vatican Council demands of us, read the signs of the times, or will it stubbornly cling to old beliefs in the face of a society that has moved on to new ways of understanding? If it refuses to change it runs the risk of becoming irrelevant.

This, as I understand it, is the nub of the problem facing the Catholic church today. Cling on to the ways and beliefs of the past, and risk becoming a small, largely irrelevant, sect. Or face the challenge of adapting its teachings to the new realities of life, with all the risks that go with that course of action, of losing what is essential.

Collapsing Institutions

We are undoubtedly living in new times, in a world that presents greater challenges than any generation before us had to face. In these times an ancient organisation like the Catholic church can provide stability and security to people who are unsettled by what is happening around them. The popularity of very traditionalist Catholic movements would appear to suggest that there are people who are looking for just such security. But, precisely because of its age, the church can have difficulty meeting the challenge of our times. In our time my contemporaries and I have seen enormous upheavals. In particular we have seen many big institutions and belief systems collapse and disintegrate. Colonialism, with all the moral and philosophical justification that sustained it for centuries, has almost disappeared. Nazism, with its belief in the supremacy of the Aryan race, was overcome after a short, though horrible, existence. Communism, which seemed so secure and stable, claiming to be based on the philosophy of Karl Marx, and with powerful armies and political structures to sustain it, imploded on itself in a dramatic way. Thankfully, apartheid is gone in the country which most typified it, due mainly to the powerful charisma of one old man. In my own little island we have seen the decay of unionism, and observed republicanism in a state of some confusion. Democracy too has its problems around the world. In many countries it has been shown to be riddled with corruption. Big and powerful media corporations have taken sides in elections in some countries, and would appear, through the use of their many outlets, to be able to influence the result. Many young people are disillusioned, and often don't bother to vote. As more and more people are asking questions about who has the real power, and the number voting in elections is declining, the whole future of democracy comes into question.

In this context I believe it is fair to ask if the Catholic church can survive. I know that even to ask this question will sound preposterous, even sacrilegious, to some. They will point to its divine origin, and the promise of Jesus that he would be with his church until the end of time. They will also point to the long history of the church, and all the revolutions, upheavals and crises it endured, and say that, having survived so much in the past, it is incapable of destruction. I don't think that on either point the answer is quite so clear-cut.

The New Testament does not state clearly that Jesus intended to found a church. Even if he did intend that a church be founded to preserve his message, it is too much to conclude that the church we have today is the blueprint he had in mind. Jesus may well continue to be with his followers without necessarily being with the present system that makes up the institutional Catholic church. And to suggest that because the church survived so many difficult times in the past, it will also survive this time which is seeing the collapse of so many great institutions, is a belief based more on hope than reality. It is questionable to say that the church, for instance, survived the Reformation, or indeed the era of revolutions. It continued on, certainly, but it was diminished by its response to these crises. Its reaction to the Reformation was antagonistic and aggressive, and the dogma and teaching that emerged in the next half-century, particularly from the Council of Trent, were far too greatly influenced by the church's desire to defeat the reformers. To use a modern phrase, much of the teaching of that time, and of that council, was agenda driven. It was aimed more at refuting the reformers than at expounding the truth. The consequences have affected the church down to our time. The revolutions, especially the one in France, frightened the church so much that it turned in on itself for centuries, and suffered massively as a result. So it is questionable how well the church survived in the past. If survival today means remaining as an institution that is trapped in its past, cut off from any meaningful interaction with the modern world, as is certainly happening to some extent, it is of no use. That type of church, as I've said, would become increasingly irrelevant; a church made up of a small group of dedicated followers who, as they increasingly lose touch with life, would come to resemble a sect.

I know that there are many people in the church who look at the modern world and feel that it has gone seriously wrong. People are more greedy, violence against the person is common and many are afraid in their homes, sexuality is debased through pornography. If this is what progress means, they want to return to the values of the past. They supported Pope John Paul II, and the Vatican establishment, in their efforts to resist change. Of course we need to retain what was good in the past, but it has to be refined to meet the new challenges of our time.

I believe that if the church is to survive as the custodian of the vibrant, life-giving teaching of Jesus, it will need to be flexible like never before, listening to the signs of the times, in dialogue with the modern world, and willing to change where new knowledge and understanding calls for change.

Reform of the System

This book is precisely that, a call for change. After forty years as a member of a religious order, and thirty as a priest, I haven't lost faith in the teaching of Christ, and his essential message for the world. I can still stand on a pulpit and speak with conviction. I know that humanity has the same longing for love, for meaning, and ultimately for everlasting life, that it always had. In some ways, in a world swamped by consumerism and materialistic values, Christ's promise of 'the fullness of life' is more relevant than ever before.

But, as I explained in the introduction, I now have difficulty with an assumption that I made automatically for a great part of my life, that in terms of teaching, Christ and the church are one and the same. I no longer accept as automatically true the belief that the church we have now is necessarily according to the plan of God. In the course of the book I will point out some ways in which the present structure of the church is more the result of power struggles down the ages than any divine inspiration.

History clearly shows that the Christian church has not always reflected the teaching of Jesus. Sometimes it has behaved in ways that were contrary to what Christ taught and the values by which he lived. The church is in constant need of reform, today as much as ever before. But history also shows that it has resisted efforts at reform in the past, and I fear it is doing the same again. It contains within its structure a strong core of establishment thinking which has succeeded in holding on to power and blocking any effort at reforming the system. I believe it is systemic reform that is needed most of all, meaning a change of the structures and systems that govern the church and by which it operates.

There are many Christian believers who hold that we no longer need a church, in the sense of an institutional structure. I am not one of those. I recently listened to a middle-aged married man giving a talk at a youth mass. He was a famous sportsman in his younger days, and the young people looked up to him as something of a hero, and gave him their full attention. He spoke about what the mass means to him. He stressed the community aspect of it. He goes to a small church in his local area, and there he meets his neighbours and friends. It means a lot to him, he said, to share this Sunday morning hour of prayer and celebration with them. Listening to him I realised that he was touching on a central aspect of the Christian faith, and a major argument for the necessity of a church. We need some form of structure in order to bring us together. We also need it as the vehicle and custodian of the message. But structures have an unfortunate habit of developing into rigid institutions, and that is where the problem lies. A structure has to be in the service of the message, not the other way round. When a particular form of church institution becomes more important than the message it is serving or the people who make it up, it is no longer fulfilling its purpose. There are many indications that we are living in such a time. In the face of a clear call for reform at the Second Vatican Council, the central core of the church institution fought to hold on to its power and successfully resisted the efforts at change. In the face of dreadful scandals of abuse by church officials the institution closed in on itself, and tried to cover up what was going on – 'for the sake of the good name of the church'. These are disturbing developments, indications of a church that has lost its way.

A New Form of Openness

I am suggesting that the way forward for the church involves a new form of openness, a willingness to allow the free flow of ideas and listening at all levels in the church. Fundamentally what is needed is a renewed faith in the presence of the Spirit of God, not just with the pope and the Vatican structure, not even confined to the bishops and priests, but present in all the faithful, indeed in the whole world. This message is preached in most parishes but when it comes to actually putting it into practice, the Vatican appropriates to itself the sole wisdom of the Holy Spirit. Historically, apart from a short period at the beginning, the church never really allowed for the presence of the Spirit outside of the authority structure. It could be said that because of this the church went wrong at a very early stage. In many different ways through the centuries the church authority imposed its views through force and coercion. Thankfully we no longer torture or put to death people who disagree with us, as they did during the centuries of the Inquisition. But has that way of thinking really changed? Hans Kung, in his book *Christianity, the Religious Situation of our Time*, suggests that things are actually not that different, that in reality little has changed:

> The Roman Inquisition, founded in the Middle Ages, continues. Its name has been changed (Holy Office, now Sacred Congregation for the Doctrine of the Faith), but essentially it still acts in accordance with the same mediaeval principles, which have little to do with generally recognised legal principles. Indeed they have little to do with the most primitive requirements of justice. This is because:
>
> • proceedings against the suspect or the accused are secret;
> • no one knows who the informants are;

- there is no cross-examination of witnesses or those laying charges;
- no inspection of documents is allowed;
- prosecutor and judge are identical;
- appeal to an independent court is either ruled out or useless;
- the aim of the inquiry is not to discover the truth but to achieve submission to Roman doctrine, which is always identical with the truth.

The question is: what does such an inquisition, which very often leads to the spiritual torture and psychological burning of those entangled in such procedures, have to do with the message and behaviour of Jesus of Nazareth? Clearly nothing at all.

The type of mentality described by Kung, this way of running the church, was never according to the mind of Christ. This book is one small effort at raising the issues, at trying to generate discussion, and, I hope, giving the Holy Spirit a chance to be heard. I don't for a moment suggest that I have the whole truth. Nothing of the kind. But I believe that the Holy Spirit can speak through me and maybe it is possible that the Spirit will say something in these pages that might be important for the future of the church.

Fear and Arrogance

Even a casual study of church history reveals two major faults that have been prevalent in the church for long periods in its history. It has displayed a high degree of arrogance, and it has used fear as a means of propagating its message. Any reform of the church must involve an effort to eradicate both of these. First we need to abolish the use of fear to keep people submissive. An institution that is custodian of the message of Christ should not be afraid of free speech, or of new ideas. What we are guardians of is not a weak philosophy that can be blown aside by the latest idea. It is the message of eternal life, and it contains answers to the questions of life like no other philosophy before or since. We do not need to silence the questions, or excommunicate the questioners. Let us trust in the power of our answers, and even more let us trust that the Spirit is present in all believers. Neither do we need to use fear in order to keep people in the church, to keep them believing. We do not need to tell people that unless they believe what we preach they will suffer the fires of hell forever. Jesus did not coerce anyone into faith, and neither should we.

Arrogance is a strange vice for a church that is built on the message of Jesus Christ. But it is a pervasive attitude that is hard to eradicate. For centuries Catholics believed that the church had all the truth, that everyone outside the church was in error, and that there was no salvation for those who were not believers in all that the Catholic church teaches. We don't need to bolster up our faith by dismissing every other point of view. The mystery of life and of God is greater and more wonderful than any mind or creed, even Christianity, can fully contain. We should be open to the possibility of learning from others, from the teaching and practice of other Christian churches, from the wisdom of the east, from the insights of modern thought. There is no such thing as a complete package of revealed truth. There is always the possibility of more insight. The breath of the Spirit blows where it will. We cannot, and neither should we want to, control it. If we can sharpen our attention to its message we can continue to advance in wisdom, age and grace. That is surely what God wishes for us as individuals, and for the whole church.

In this book I will look first of all at the way the church developed, and how the structures came into being, with particular emphasis on the development of the practice of authority within the church. This is where I think the biggest problem lies. Power and decision-making in the church is centralised in the hands of a small group of people who are answerable to nobody. There is far too much secrecy. Few if any outside the Vatican seem to know how the system works, who really makes the decisions, and

how they can be influenced. This is certainly not the way it was
at the beginning. Over the centuries the pope has gradually become more powerful and has assumed a profile that I believe is not
healthy for the church as a whole. I will give particular attention
to the period from the Protestant Reformation to the middle of
the twentieth century, because it was a time when it seems to me
that the church went seriously wrong in significant ways.

Then I will take up some of the burning issues where I think
change is urgently needed. Ministry is clearly one of these, and I
will deal with the notion of priesthood, and how our present system is no longer serving the church as it should. The attitude of
the church to women is gradually becoming a major source of unhappiness, and indeed scandal, and it will continue to be so until
something is done to change the present situation. I will give
some of the historical background, and point to ways forward.
The church has never distinguished itself in its teaching on sex,
and today, for various reasons, it has lost a great deal of credibility in this area. I will attempt to explain why, and where we have
gone wrong. Confession has been one of the flash points of the
exercise of power in the church, and is in something of a flux at
the moment. I will suggest where we need to go with this sacrament. I will look at particular teachings, for instance infallibility,
the virgin birth, the Immaculate Conception, compulsory celibacy for priests, and suggest that maybe we need to re-think them.

There are some who believe that the church does not need to
change, or that it has already changed too much. From what I
have already written it is obvious I am not one of those. I am very
much in agreement with John Henry Newman who believed that
change was an essential aspect of life. In the following chapters I
will outline the changes that I believe are needed.

II

THE CHURCH AND
THE EXERCISE OF AUTHORITY

Many non-Christians have had critical things to say about the Catholic church down through the centuries. Gandhi's oft quoted statement, how he liked our Christ but didn't particularly like Christians, because to him we seemed to be too unlike Christ, is probably the best known. The philosopher Kirkegaard put it this way:

> Christendom has done away with Christianity, without being quite aware of it. The consequence is that, if anything is to be done, one must try again to introduce Christianity into Christendom.

Whether or not we fully accept Kirkegaard's assessment of us, I'm sure most people will agree that the challenge he puts before us contains a very strong element of truth for our generation of Christians. How can we re-introduce Christianity into Christendom?

In any society or institution the question of who controls the levers of power is important. In the most recent presidential election in the United States the candidates spent countless millions to acquire a job that pays less than half a million dollars per year. The lure was power, to be in charge of the most powerful nation in the world. It would be foolish to think that the church, because its *raison d'être* is religious, would be free from the power struggles that are common in other institutions.

I want to look at the way the church has developed over the

two millennia of its existence, how it built up its present structures and system of government. I will try to examine in particular
how the church has exercised power and authority down through
the centuries and to what extent it may have been corrupted by
power. In other words, I'm asking if Christendom has lost its
Christianity.

The Example of Jesus
In thinking about the church it is crucial that we try to keep our
sights set on Jesus, the type of person he was and the message he
preached. We can never afford to forget the origin of the church
and from where it draws its message. Anybody in a position of
authority in the church should never allow the New Testament
far from their sight. 'I have come not to be served, but to serve'.
Sentences like that should act as a cor-rective to the person who
has his or her sights set on a position of power in the church. The
story of the temptations of Jesus is very instructive, since it can
be interpreted as giving us a picture of Jesus' attitude to power
and control. I presume the story, as it has come down to us, is not
an accurate historical account, but came from a community of believers who wanted to give us a picture of Jesus and of his teaching. Rather than all these temptations happening in one se-
quence over the course of a few hours, it is more likely that the
story sums up the temptations faced by Jesus in the course of his
ministry. That does not in any way diminish the truth of the message contained in the story. Jesus was tempted, and the temptations he endured were the very human ones that each of us experience in our lives. As the story goes, the first temptation was
greed: 'bid these stones turn into loaves of bread'. Every human
being, irrespective of their economic circumstances, has suffered
this temptation. Jesus gives that wonderful answer: 'A person does
not live on bread alone, but on every word that comes from the
mouth of God'. The second temptation was to his faith and belief

in the goodness of God: from the highest point of the temple he was invited to throw himself down, to see if God would save him. But he rejects this too, on the basis that one should not put God to the test. The third temptation is the one that most concerns me in this chapter. Jesus is presented with the lure and attraction of power. The tempter offers him control over all the kingdoms of the world, on condition that he bow down and worship him. This must have been a big temptation to Jesus as a human person. The story recognises that power is one of the great temptations for everyone. It is not just people in positions of authority in state and church that exercise power. We all have the capacity to exercise power over others in all sorts of ways, subtle or otherwise. The abuse of power demeans both the person who abuses it, and the people who are abused. Just as the condition the tempter made was that Jesus would worship him in return for all this power, a person or institution that becomes corrupted by power is in the grip of a particularly pernicious form of evil. Jesus rejected that last temptation of the tempter ('you must worship the Lord, your God, and serve him alone'), and all through his life he turned his back on power in the many different ways it presented itself to him. His followers, when they came to believe that he was the promised Messiah, wanted to make him king of the Jews. As he entered Jerusalem the people hailed him as their king. But he refused it all. Just before he died he told Pilate that his kingdom was not of this world. Even when he exercised his spiritual power, for instance in healing and raising people from the dead, he tried to keep it quiet. When he healed the two blind men in Matthew's Gospel, he said: 'Don't tell anyone about this!' As if they were going to keep quiet about the momentous fact that they had got their sight back. But he clearly wanted his message to stand on its own, to be accepted or rejected by people in freedom, taking it at its own value. Of course the men talked. The Gospel says they 'spread the news about Jesus all over that part of the country'. So this was the attitude of Christ; everything was by invitation, nothing by coercion. Let us look now at how well the church has imitated Jesus in this aspect of his life and ministry, and what lessons are there for us in our time. The Russian novelist, Fyodor Dostoevsky, in his classic novel *The Brothers Karamazov*, tells a story of Jesus coming back to Seville in the sixteenth century and being confronted by the 'grand inquisitor', the medieval equivalent of the cardinal secretary of the Congregation for the Doctrine of the Faith. In the debate between them the grand inquisitor tells Jesus that he made a fatal mistake in not accepting the three offers of the tempter. He refused these offers because he wanted people to accept him in freedom. The inquisitor asserts that people are not capable of freedom; that they must be treated as slaves.

The purpose of the church is fundamentally quite simple. For believers it is the custodian of the greatest message that the world has ever heard, the message of new life Jesus brought to humanity. The work of the church is to preserve and promote Christ's message, and to be a means by which people can access Jesus and his gift of life. In other words, the church is there to be of service both to the message and to the people. This is an absolutely fundamental point, and we must try to keep it in mind, and constantly to measure the church against it. It is important for us that the church be as close to perfect in its service as it possibly can. But of course we would be fools to think that perfection can ever be attained in this world, even by the church!

Did Jesus Found a Church?
Let us begin with a fairly fundamental question. Did Jesus found a church, and if he did, is the Catholic church as it exists today the church that he wished to found?

How you answer this question will be greatly influenced by the way in which you interpret the New Testament, and in particular the four Gospels. If you believe, like some Protestant fundamentalists, that the Gospels are precise and accurate accounts of the actions and words of Jesus, then you will take some of the sentences about founding a church, and interpret them to mean that Jesus had a clear idea of what he wanted, and that is represented in today's Christian church. You will, of course, have problems about all the different churches within the Christian tradition, and the deep bitterness and division between them. Did he found them all, or only the particular one that you happen to belong to? Did he intend this great diversity of Christian groups, with all the quarrels and rivalry between them? When he prayed that they may all be one, did he want all his followers to be part of the one institution? There are many questions.

Most Catholic Scripture scholars take a different view of the Gospels. They do not see them as accurate historical accounts of the life and teaching of Jesus. Instead, they emerged from what is known as the 'post-resurrection' church, and were written down in the later years of the first century. As such, they have to be interpreted within the context out of which they were produced. A good illustration of this is the sentence from Matthew's Gospel, where Jesus is quoted as telling his disciples to 'baptise them in the name of the Father and of the Son and of the Holy Spirit'. The Jewish religion strongly believed in the notion of one God, in contrast to the pagans around them, who believed in many gods. It was only gradually that the church worked out the concept of the Trinity, in order to retain the belief in one God, while allowing for the Son and the Holy Spirit. The idea of the Trinity as expressed in this sentence could not have been used by Jesus. It would have been completely foreign to Jewish belief and expression, and Jesus was a Jew. So it was clearly added much later to include and affirm the new teaching of the Trinity.

The weight of evidence suggests that Jesus didn't have anything as specific as a church in mind. He gave his followers a mission, to go and preach the Kingdom of God, but he didn't set up or outline any type of structure. Even if he did intend some form of institutional framework, we cannot be certain what system he had in mind. He most definitely didn't spell it out. At the same time it is a firm belief of all Christians that Jesus is with his followers, and that he will continue to be with believers until the end of time. But what exactly does that mean? It doesn't mean that the church, or church leaders, suddenly becomes more than human, no longer subject to the fallibility and weakness of human nature. Down through history certain popes and bishops were inclined to believe that they had superior powers. This is illustrated best in the belief that the church can never make a mistake, can never be in error, a belief that can be seen as damaging, and which I will discuss later. It will help to look at some aspects of the development of the early church, and see something of how the present structures and power-systems that we have developed.

Early Christian Communities

The church began very simply. The apostles and the other close followers of Jesus, after they had come to the gradual realisation that Christ was not dead and gone, but that he had risen and was still with them, found their courage again, spread out and began to preach and tell stories about Jesus. Gradually they gathered small communities about them, and these were the earliest forms of church in the Christian sense. Most of the apostles worked initially among the Jews. Paul, who wasn't one of the original disciples of Jesus, was probably the most effective of all in terms of spreading the message, and forming a church. He, with Barnabas and others, went to preach to the Greek communities, in places like Antioch, Corinth and Ephesus. This was presumably a very deliberate decision on his part. While Rome was the political capital of the world at the time, Greece was very much the intellectual centre. So, from the beginning there were two quite distinct types of community in the church; those formed among the Jews, and the Pauline communities, mostly Greek, though located in Asia Minor. The Acts of the Apostles give some indication of the tensions between them. What is significant from our point of view is that those early communities did not have any central government, most especially the ones formed by Paul. They were made up of a whole variety of ministries. St Paul explains the thinking behind it:

> There are different abilities to perform service, but the same God gives ability to everyone for their service. The Spirit gives one a message of wisdom, while to another the same Spirit gives a message of knowledge. One and the same Spirit gives faith to one, while to another he gives the power to heal. The Spirit gives one the power to work miracles, to another the gift of speaking God's message, and to yet another the ability to tell the difference between gifts that come from the Spirit and those that do not. To one he gives the ability to speak in strange tongues, and to another the ability to explain what is said. But it is one and the same Spirit who does all this; he gives a different gift to each person, as he wishes (1 Cor. 12).

This appears to me to be a crucial passage from St Paul. It gives a picture of a community comprising many different gifts and talents, all of which are at the service of the community, and are used by the community for the good of everyone. The community is at the heart of it all, and the idea of service is central. Paul also clearly believes that the Spirit is active among all the believers rather than just the leaders. Only gradually as the message spread did there seem to be a need for some more clear-cut form of leadership. This was the stage at which the community dimension of the early churches began to decline. The various different ministries gradually came to be subsumed into one. A clear leader of the community began to emerge. In the Jewish structure priests were the ones who serviced the temple. After the collapse of the

Jewish priesthood with the destruction of the temple in 70 AD, the Christian communities slowly took over the word 'priest', and applied it to their leaders. This was mostly a second-century development. As it progressed, and as authority became more focused, the centrality of the community weakened. The emphasis shifted to the person in charge rather than the whole group. This change is immensely significant for the later history of the church.

Centralisation

Close on 300 years had passed from the time of Jesus before the real centralising and institutionalising of the church began in earnest. This was when the Christian church became the official religion of the Roman Empire, under the Emperor Constantine in the fourth century. The writers Michael Baigent and Richard Leigh, in their book *Holy Blood, Holy Grail*, suggest that Constantine substantially reshaped Christian teaching and practice at this time, particularly removing the feminine element from it, and suppressing facts about the life of Jesus, especially his supposed marriage to Mary Magdalene. Dan Brown's enormously popular novel, *The Da Vinci Code*, is based on that idea. I don't intend going down that road. It seems to me that the evidence for those claims is fairly thin, though it will be obvious from reading my book that I agree with some aspects of what they are suggesting.

Rome, being the centre of the empire, was also the obvious place for the headquarters of church government. Consequently the church in Rome had a certain claim to authority. From the beginning it drew on the Roman talent for organisation and an understanding of how politics worked. It gradually came to model itself on the structures of the civil government. Even the rituals and forms of dress owe a great deal to the empire. The ceremonial dress of bishops, cardinals and popes would not have seemed at all out of place in those days, because they were similar enough to the way Roman officials dressed. But of course the Roman Empire

decayed and fell apart a few centuries later, while the church structures that were modelled on it remain to this day. What was normal ceremonial dress 1,500 years ago now seems anachronistic.

In the context of the issues I am dealing with in this book it
is very important to point out that in those early centuries there
was no question of the Roman church having any legal primacy
or authority over the other communities of believers that had
sprung up around Europe, the Middle East and North Africa, and
that also called themselves churches. Even Augustine, the greatest theologian of the first millennium, who lived in the fifth century, did not see the bishop of Rome as having any special authority. For him all bishops were equal in principle. The Latin phrase
that was used for most of the first millennium to describe the
position of the bishop of Rome in relation to the other churches
was *primus inter pares*, the first among equals. The bishop of Rome
had a special position, but that did not give him authority over
all the others. They were all equal.

The Primacy of Rome

The notion of Rome as what was called the 'primatial see', the
one with authority over everyone else, began to gather momen-
tum early in the second millennium. It got its big impetus during
the reign of Pope Gregory VII. He was a man of great strength
and ability, who carried out some much needed reform in the
church. He believed strongly in developing the papacy into the
central authority. He made out a list of statements about the importance of his position as pope. It is known as the 'Dictates of
the Pope', a list of twenty-five statements. Some of them are worth
quoting. They give a flavour of his thinking. After what we have
experienced of the centralised focus on the pope during the reign
of Pope John Paul II, the first few dictates might not seem strange,
but at the time they were a significant change from the form of
church government prevalent for the first 1,000 years:

- Only the bishop of Rome is legitimately called universal bishop.
- He alone can depose or reinstate bishops.
- He alone is permitted to decree new laws, establish new bishoprics.
- He alone may use imperial insignia.
- All rulers have to kiss the pope's feet.
- His name is unique in the world.
- He is permitted to depose emperors.
- He himself may not be judged by anyone.
- The Roman church has never erred, and according to the testimony of scripture will never ever err.

Reading that list of dictates it is hard to avoid the conclusion that Gregory had a very different attitude to power than Christ, and the message of the dictates is in sharp contrast to a lot of what is in the Gospels. It also, of course, put paid to Augustine's notion of *primus inter pares*. Gregory didn't see anybody as equal to himself. He was clearly modelling himself on the temporal rulers, the kings and emperors of his day. Ultimate power was the objective. It is hard to see how he could reconcile his desire to have all other rulers kiss his feet with Christ who washed the feet of his disciples, and who said that whoever wanted to make himself great must become the last of all and the servant of all. His last dictate, that the Roman church has never erred, rings a bit hollow in the context of the other dictates. By drawing up a list of statements about how powerful he was, he was already deeply in error in relation to the teaching of Christ.

A century or so later Pope Innocent III, who became pope in 1198, went even further in establishing and reinforcing papal power and authority. In his sermon on the day of his consecration he described himself 'as the representative of Christ set between God and human beings, below God and above human beings, less than God and more than human beings, judge of all and to be judged by no one, except the Lord'.

Clearly at this stage the papacy had, in modern terminology, lost the run of itself. Power had gone to their heads, and they had forgotten the real nature of the person they were representing. Innocent III seemed to see himself as some form of superhuman being, above everyone else. It was an amazing and unfortunate development.

During all of this period and right down to the middle of the nineteenth century, the papacy was also a civil power, ruling a large part of central Italy, known as the Papal States. I know that in the context of history there was a certain justification for this, in terms of providing defence and security for the office of the papacy. But it is another illustration of how far removed from the Christ whose 'kingdom is not of this world' the church had strayed. The representative of Christ on earth should never have been a civil ruler. A lot of the authoritarianism, the large civil service, the pomp and ceremony of the present day Vatican have their origin in the fact of the civil government.

Readers may be inclined to look on all of this as no more than interesting historical detail. It is much more than that. Because of the nature of the church, and the great emphasis it places on tradition, these historical figures have actually had a major say in defining the type of church we have today. If we are to make any headway in changing the system, we must understand where it came from, and how it developed as it did.

Pope Versus Council

Besides the pope, who as we see has been growing in authority and power over the centuries, the other system of government within the church was a council. This was a gathering of bishops and other authority figures, together with the pope, to discuss the issues of the time. Many councils had been held during the first millennium. There was quite a power struggle between the authority of councils and that of the pope. All through the second millennium this same debate continued. Who had ultimate autho-

rity? Was it an ecumenical council, or was it the pope? Many of
the great minds of those centuries concerned themselves with the
topic, which shows that they recognised how important it was.
One of the greatest teachers, Thomas Aquinas, was an enthusi-
astic supporter of the power of the papacy. Contrary to Augustine, who believed that the council, the assembly of the church
leaders, was the supreme authority, Thomas Aquinas argued that
it was the pope, and that he alone could convene a council. Two
statements of his in particular have been of great use to the papal
side in the debate on the primacy of the pope. He said that 'it is
for the pope to define what faith is'.

That certainly gave him substantial power, because it was
power over people's minds. In any society control over the belief
system is essential to retaining power. But as a consequence debate about truth suffers because the power system cannot afford
to be open to different ideas. But Thomas Aquinas' other statement is even stronger: 'It is necessary for salvation to submit to
the Roman pope'.

Here we have the beginnings of emotional and psychological
fear, which became so much a feature of Catholic church teaching in later centuries. It is also the origin of a teaching that came
down to our time, but is generally disregarded in this age of ecumenism – that outside the church there is no salvation; in other
words, that everyone who is not a Catholic is excluded from
Heaven. Not long afterwards this was defined as a doctrine by
Pope Boniface VIII in the Bull *Unam Sanctam* (1302) in the context of a power struggle with the French king, Philip IV. Here we
see something that has bedevilled the church down through history. A doctrine that was later to prove problematic was promulgated in the context of a dispute, as a means of winning an argument against opponents.

The two great popes of papal primacy, Gregory VII and Innocent III, must have been dancing with delight in their graves

at these statements from Aquinas, and at the Bull of Pope Boniface. The papacy had effectively won the argument. Power was in its hands. It is only fair to mention here that Thomas Aquinas was probably the greatest theologian and scholar that the church has known, and that we all owe an enormous debt to him for his scholarship and wisdom. But even he was not free from error.

The Significance of the Council of Constance

In the fifteenth century there was an effort, at the Council of Constance (1415) to change the balance of power. This council came at the end of a period of division or schism, known as the Babylonian captivity of the papacy, in which there were two, and for a short while, three popes. This schism developed out of the decision of Pope Clement V, a Frenchman, to take up his residence in Avignon rather than in Rome in the early part of the fourteenth century. Eventually the Council of Constance was convened because the divisions had got so deep that there were now three popes, and an effort was being made to solve the problem. The council deposed all three, and appointed a new one, Martin V, and the schism ended. This was immensely significant. A council of the church had deposed a pope. That seemed to clearly establish the fact that a council of the whole church has authority over the pope. It is worth quoting the actual text of the decree of that council:

> Duly assembled in the Holy Spirit, forming a general council, and representing the Catholic church, the synod has its authority from Christ. Thus everyone of whatever estate or dignity, even the papal dignity, has to obey it in all that concerns the faith, the overcoming of the said schism and the reform of this church, head and members.

It also decreed that all future popes should regularly convene general councils, and that the council, not the pope, was the custodian of the church's well-being, and the instrument of reform.

Unfortunately it made very little difference in practice; there was a major gap between theory and practice. The movement to-wards papal primacy and centralised authority continued. As the historian, Eamon Duffy, puts it:

> the 'politics of oblivion' got under way, as Roman theologians and apologists began rewriting history. The distinguished American church historian Francis Oakley explains how what he calls a laun-dering of the collective memory took place. In the *Dictionary of Catholic Theology* (1911) there is a list of the general councils of the Catholic church. This list passes straight from the Council of Vienna (1311) to the Council of Florence (1439). Most readers would prob-ably miss the fact that no fewer than three early-fifteenth-century assemblies, long accepted as general councils of the Catholic church, had been quietly edited out. These were the councils of Pisa, Basel and, most significantly of all, the Council of Constance (*Priests and People*, April 2004).

To recognise the Council of Constance would make arguments for centralised papal authority hard to sustain. The easiest thing to do was to pretend that it never happened.

The movement for papal primacy reached its highest point with the First Vatican Council in the middle of the nineteenth century. This was called by Pope Pius IX. His purpose was to estab-lish for all time the pope as the supreme authority, above all oth-ers. In other words, he wanted to end the debate as to where the authority lay. In order to do that he needed increased power, so he wanted to have papal infallibility declared a doctrine of the faith. This is the doctrine that is commonly understood to mean that the pope cannot make a mistake. It is fair to say that this has caused considerable controversy, and has widened the divisions between the Christian churches. Indeed it was controversial even at the time. There was deep division within the council. The opponents of the move, mostly the German and French bishops, staged a walk-out before the vote was taken. I will deal with this doctrine in more detail later.

The Second Vatican Council

The next major gathering of the church was in the 1960s, at the Second Vatican Council. This was called a council of reform, and one of its aims was to reform the structures of the church. There were two main ways in which this council attempted to reform the system of government. Firstly the bishops wanted to reform the Curia, and particularly what was known as the Sanctum Officium, the Sacred Office. The Curia could be called the civil service of the church, and the Sacred Office was the strongest and most influential section of the Curia. It mainly concerned itself with discipline and the preservation of orthodoxy. It decided what could and could not be believed. It was most notorious for being the body within the Vatican that implemented such policies as the Inquisition and the syllabus of errors. Paul VI, the pope during the later part of the council, did make an attempt at reforming the Curia. He started out with a fair degree of enthusiasm, calling the Curia together in September 1963, and putting forward significant proposals for reform:

> We must accept with humility the criticisms which surround us, with reflection and also with gratitude. Rome has no need to defend itself by making itself deaf to suggestions that come to it from honest voices, especially when they are those of friends and brothers.

But unfortunately it did prove deaf, and as time went on Paul VI's enthusiasm waned, and in the end his reform amounted to little more than a reorganisation, with no diminution of power. He renamed the Sacred Office as the Congregation for the Doctrine of the Faith, and for a while it lost some of its power to control, but unfortunately during the pontificate of Pope John Paul II it was probably more powerful than ever, with our present pope, the then Cardinal Joseph Ratzinger at its head.

The second idea of the Vatican Council members was to set up a council of bishops. This was to be a body that would meet regularly and, somewhat like a parliament in the democratic system, would assist the pope in governing the church. With the powerful position of the Curia it was as if the civil service was running a country. The structure envisioned by the council was that the pope would be advised by the council of bishops rather than the Curia in his major decision-making. This would be the legislative body, and the Curia would function more as an executive body, implementing the decisions made by the pope and council of bishops. Unfortunately this idea, even though it had the support of the large majority of bishops attending the council, did not get approval. Many a battle took place on the council floor, as are recorded in Hans Kung's memoirs, My Struggle for Freedom, but the end result was that the Curia managed to block reform, and retain its power. As a compromise a synod of bishops was set up, but this has proved almost totally ineffective. It does not meet regularly, but only when called together by the pope. The agenda is set by Rome rather than the bishops, and, most telling of all, the final report from the synod is written by the pope after it concludes. So the synod is almost totally powerless. The Curia still rules supreme. This whole struggle for reform was to all intents and purposes a political battle, and the bureaucrats won. Since then their power has increased greatly. In fact it is ironic, in the papacy of someone who travelled widely and was very popular, the church became more centralised and autocratic under Pope John Paul II than it has been for a long time.

Hans Kung, in the memoirs referred to above, makes a very interesting point about both John XXIII and Paul VI, the two popes who presided at the Second Vatican Council. Both were in favour of reform, but were ultimately cautious men, and their caution became their undoing. While speaking about and apparently supporting reform, they appointed to the top posts in the Curia people who were totally opposed to reform. Kung says this is particularly true of Paul VI. He became pope during the council. There was immense support among the bishops attending the council for the reform of the Curia. A large majority of them would have enthusiastically endorsed any move in that direction. Paul VI himself apparently wanted it, if we can believe his public statements. He had a unique opportunity. With the death of a pope all Curial offices become vacant, and have to be filled by his successor. The supporters of reform were appalled by the fact that Paul VI reappointed all the old faces, including the eighty-two-year-old Cardinal Cicognani as secretary of state. So Paul, like John before him, didn't quite have the courage of his convictions. He wanted reforms, but he wasn't prepared to make the hard decisions in relation to personnel necessary to see those reforms through. As a consequence he surrounded himself with people who made sure that what he appeared to want to achieve would be blocked. It was a strange contradiction. It showed the side of the church as a truly human, political organisation. It often happens that a new leader, even though intent on reform, re-appoints all the old guard. They tend to justify this by saying that it is done in the interests of unity and experience. However, it is also possible that the new leader cannot stomach the conflict, the ostracisation that might ensue if a clean sweep were made. It would seem that this was particularly the case with Paul VI. In my own experience in the church I have seen similar developments both at diocesan and religious life level, where a programme of reform is put into the hands of a leader incapable and unwilling to implement it.

The Present Church Structure

So, 2,000 years after the time of Jesus, what type of church struc-ture have we got? Without going into too much detail, it has to be said that the main feature of church government is its cen-tralised nature. The Vatican is a bureaucratic body, with a long history and tradition behind it. In terms of the scale of bureau-cracy that many countries would have in their government, the Vatican system is neither large nor well-funded. But I don't be-lieve that takes away from its ability to control what happens around the world. It is secretive. The processes and forms of deci-sion-making are unknown to those outside. It would be hard to find any other institution or system that has such a centralised government as the Catholic church. Some of the communist coun-tries of the last century had it, but they did not last. It is modelled firstly on the Roman empire and then on the medieval autocratic monarchies, and there is little element of democracy about it. The pope acts as the supreme ruler. All final decisions belong to him. The Vatican retains total authority over church teaching, discipline and appointments. The inner circle consists of a body of cardinals with the pope as their head. This is the Curia.

Working out from this solid centralised body, each individual diocese around the world is ruled by a bishop, all of whom are now appointed by the pope. It is only in the last 100 years or so that the pope has control of all appointments. Before that many bishops were elected, or in some cases appointed by the local lord, which was also a dubious practice. There is a very limited and secretive form of consultation conducted by the papal nuncio of the particular country before the appointment of a bishop, but many feel that it is meaningless, and some priests (it is impossible to know how many because it is all a secret) refuse to take part in the process any more. A bishop has a certain amount of authority in his diocese, particularly over his priests. The main power he has over them is that he can move them around at will; and that power has often been used by bishops as a means of silencing out-spoken priests, and disciplining recalcitrant ones. I recently came across a situation where a priest in a parish was very unhappy about the policy being pursued by the bishop, and the way he had treated one of his fellow priests. I asked him if he had made known his feelings to the bishop. He said no, he had not. He explained his position as follows: 'I am due a change in two years' time; I will be of age to get my first parish. I am in no position to alienate the bishop!'

In some dioceses there is a priest's council, and a degree of consultation goes on about the appointment of priests to parishes. In others, the bishop decides himself, and notifies the priest of his new posting. In no instance that I am aware of are the people of the parish consulted about who will minister to them as their priest. Mostly there isn't much real communication between the bishop and the ordinary people of the diocese. He is usually a fairly remote figure, who comes to the parish once a year, normally to administer the sacrament of confirmation. That is a formal and highly structured occasion, which does not lend itself to any real discussion between bishop and people. In normal circumstances the line of communication between an ordinary Catholic and his bishop is through the priest. The fact that bishops often live in large houses with imposing entrances adds to their distance from the people. During the reign of Pope John Paul II we saw the appointment of a particular type of person as a bishop. These were often academics, who had spent their lives in seminaries or universities, and had little or no pastoral experience. They were also often cautious people, who were put into the position because they were regarded as being 'safe', men who would not do anything foolish or in any way unorthodox. Orthodoxy, particularly in relation to the church's sexual teaching, the question of the ordination of women, and more recently the practice of confession, is a big issue in today's Catholic church. It was hardly a word that was used about Jesus during his years of public ministry. In just about every way you could think of, Jesus was different and decidedly unorthodox. It is ironic that the church which claims him as founder has now become obsessed with orthodoxy. The easiest way to be orthodox is to keep your head down and do little or nothing, and that is very much a feature of leadership in the church at present. But in reality, apart from his power over his priests, the bishop has little enough actual authority. Everything he does has to be in conformity with Rome. So he has to constantly look over his shoulder, and if he steps out of line in any way he will be quickly reprimanded. The only type of person who will think and act independently as a bishop in today's church is someone who is completely devoid of personal ambition. Someone who is ambitious for promotion is totally under the thumb of Rome, because unless he acts in accordance with their wishes he will not get his desired promotion. I recently asked a priest in a particular diocese how his bishop was doing. 'He is doing very little', he answered. 'He has his sights set on promotion.' Promotion wasn't the actual word he used. Instead he mentioned the name of the city where the archbishop lived. Thankfully there are some bishops who have that freedom in themselves, but it is also true that a substantial number of those in authority in the church are careerists, people who have ambition for promotion. It is my impression that the present administration in the Vatican has nurtured and favoured careerism. It has created an elite within the church. To quote from one of my earlier works, *The Death of Religious Life?* (1997):

> The sociologist, Thomas Bottomore, in his book, *Elites in Society*, recognises that elites always develop, but it is the closed elite that is dangerous, i.e. the one that does not allow others in, or only allows them in on condition that they accept the elite's way of doing things. This inevitably creates a sense of alienation among some, which is very detrimental to the overall morale of the group.

The present Vatican structure is one such elite, closed in on itself, and leaving many in the church with a sense of alienation.

Is Reform Possible?
What can be done about all of this? Many people believe that reform of the church is impossible. They look at all the efforts made down through the centuries, and how the structures have perpetuated themselves and resisted change. They look at the great effort made at the Second Vatican Council, and what has happened since then. The Australian writer, Morris West, describes this well:

> I was in Rome during the wonderful, hopeful years of Vatican II. Since then, I have seen the progress which was then begun – which I saw and still see as a progress of charity within the church – grind to a halt. I have seen, on the other hand, the processes of alienation quicken and more and more people standing outside the doors of the church, which seem closed against them because the cost of re-entry appears beyond their strength and the grace beyond their reach.

Morris West is not hopeful. Another, more lengthy, quote from him highlights the contrast between the simplicity of Jesus and the paraphernalia of the Catholic church:

> The irony for me is that we who follow Jesus have erected whole mountains of books over his simple teaching. We have written and sometimes forged whole volumes of decretals and canons and acts of the apostolic see and admonitions and anathemas and condemnations of death and excommunications of whole peoples – and we call it what? – the exercise of the magisterium, the exercise of the power of the keys. Let me remind you, however, that, exercising the same power, we tortured and burned men and women too, for alleged heresy, sorcery and witchcraft.
> I confess to you that the older I get, the more I am haunted by the contrasts between the two images: the dark man from Nazareth

bowed over the temple pavement, scribbling in the dust, and the huge fearsome array of hierarchies and legislators and inquisitors down the centuries, entrenched behind their mountains of documents demanding, as the price of faith, obedience to their magistracy.

The contrast creates a nightmare for many: a nightmare of alienation from Christ's own simple summary: 'By this shall all know that you are my disciples, that you have love for one another.' I tell you now, in the cold light of observable fact: we are in schism, a schism of indifference, because those who regulate the church have committed themselves to a policy of sterile legalism, instead of a policy of loving care to inform the church and revivify it with the saving Spirit of its master.

These quotes are taken from Morris West's book *A View from the Ridge*, written when he was eighty years of age, and after a lifetime of commitment to the church. It is a vibrant, faith-filled book, and yet full of anger at the institution of the church, and all the injustice it has perpetrated.

Is there hope for the future, or is the situation now so entrenched that nothing is possible? I have to believe that change is possible. Maybe I am fooling myself, but I prefer to interpret it as a stance of faith, faith that the Spirit is with the church, and if she or he is, then anything is possible. I want to make some suggestion as to what I see as essential if the church is to recapture the message of its founder, Jesus; or to put it another way, if we are to restore Christianity to Christendom.

A Way Forward

The first thing I would like to do is to rid the church for all time of this incredible and preposterous notion that it cannot make mistakes, that it is incapable of error. As I have outlined above, this idea has a long history and tradition in the church, coming to general prominence in the reign of Gregory VII in the eleventh century. It has been part of the belief system out of which the church government has operated down to our own time. How anyone can seriously assert that the church has never been in error, no matter what theological twist they might try to put on it, baffles me. Even the most cursory look at church history shows that the church has made many mistakes, done some terrible things, and has at times been deeply in error. Before we can make any progress towards real reform it is important that we recognise and acknowledge this. Apart from the blatant falseness of this stance, it is not even a sensible position to hold. To be incapable of error means by definition to be also incapable of learning, because if you assert that you cannot make mistakes, then where is the room for improvement? It is an acknowledged part of human existence that we do most of our learning from our mistakes. If the church believes that it is incapable of error, then it will never recognise the need for change. And how can one be so certain of one's own infallibility and not become arrogant? Unfortunately arrogance has been a feature of church government too often down through the ages. We need to free ourselves from all of that. Yes, we have made mistakes; many of them, and sometimes with terrible consequences for people, some as important as Galileo, others as ordinary as couples who struggled with the teaching of *Humanae Vitae*. Let us acknowledge that, and begin the slow and painful process of trying to learn from these mistakes. The scandal of child abuse within the church has been horrible. But at least it has begun to teach us humility. Out of this particular context it is not as easy for church officials to talk about never being in error.

The idea that the church can never be in error seems to have grown out of the belief that Christ remains with his church. I have no difficulty with that belief. Without him there would be no meaning at all to our faith, we would be without anything or anybody to hope in. But he does not impose his views on anyone; he does not force himself. His presence with us is not a guarantee

of perfection. Each human being is left free to choose Jesus and
his way if they wish. This applies to church leaders as much as
anybody else. As church history clearly illustrates, bishops, cardinals, popes are subject to all the same human weaknesses and
temptations as the rest of us. A person can occupy a high position
within the church and still be blinded to Christ's message by
pride, greed, weakness, hunger for power, lust, or any of the many
other human failures. Power corrupts within the church just as
much as it does in all other areas of life. It is important to face up
to the truth. The church has been in error, no doubt future generations will see clearly the errors we are making in this generation, but they too will make their own mistakes. The best we can
hope for is that, despite all our human frailty, even at times stu-
pidity, weakness and sin, the truth of Christ will come through,
and continue to set people free.

I like the way Morris West puts it:

> In the context of church history, the greatest stain upon our repu-
> tation as conservators of the gospel truth has been that it takes us
> decades and centuries to admit our mistakes.

Papal Infallibility

In my opinion the second big topic we need to take a hard look
at is the doctrine of papal infallibility and the primacy of the Roman pontiff. It is difficult to avoid the suspicion that papal infallibility was defined, in 1870 at the First Vatican Council, as an
exercise in power, an effort to increase the power of the papacy.
It is one of the great bulwarks of the centralised authority of the
Vatican, with the pope at its head. It is a doctrine that is not generally understood by the average Catholic. If I am correct there are
at least three possible interpretations prevalent in the church
today. Some think the doctrine means that the pope is infallible
in everything he does and says. Others believe that the pope is

infallible only when he declares himself to be so. Another interpretation is that the pope is only infallible when he speaks a truth
that is generally accepted both by the bishops and the consensus
of the faithful.

I know the language is difficult, but I think it is worthwhile
quoting the actual text of the definition, as it was defined at the
First Vatican Council in 1870:

> The Roman Pontiff when he speaks *ex cathedra*, that is, when, exer-
> cising the office of pastor and teacher of all Christians, he defines
> with his supreme apostolic authority a doctrine concerning faith or
> morals to be held by the universal church, through the divine assis-
> tance promised to him in blessed Peter, is possessed of that infalli-
> bility with which the divine Redeemer willed his church to be
> endowed in defining faith and morals: and therefore such definitions
> of the Roman Pontiff are irreformable of themselves (and not from
> the consent of the church).

I'm sure for the average person, not versed in the language of
church doctrine, the above definition doesn't throw much light
on the situation, but maybe it helps to show why there is so much
confusion as to what the doctrine actually means. It has been a
cause of argument and debate ever since it was defined. There
have also been disputes over whether particular statements of
popes have been infallible or not.

The two promulgations that are generally recognised as clearly
intended to be infallible have to do with Our Lady. On the first
occasion (which preceded the council, in 1854) Mary was said to
have been immaculately conceived, and the second one (1950)
declared that she was assumed, body and soul, into Heaven. Both
are problematic, particularly the first one. To say that Mary was
conceived without original sin one needs to think in terms of a
theology that is no longer prevalent in the church. It was based
on the old notion, taught by Augustine 1,500 years ago, that orig-

inal sin was a stain on the soul that was passed on from one generation to the next through the act of sexual intercourse. In that
context it was possible to imagine Mary being born with a soul
pure and free from stain. But that understanding of original sin is
no longer tenable. Modern teaching is more likely to define original sin as the human condition into which we are born, with all
the suffering, sin and evil that are part of humanity. With that
understanding it is hard to make sense of saying that Mary was
preserved free from original sin. It makes her in some way not
quite human or earthly, and I don't think either of those notions
does her much justice. She would no longer be a useful role model
for us humans, since she would have lived her life free of the pain
and struggle of humanity. It would also, of course, raise questions
about the humanity of Jesus. So this doctrine needs to be looked
at, and redefined in a way that makes sense today. Let us return
to the topic of infallibility.

In more recent times there was an attempt by the Congregation for the Doctrine of the Faith in the Vatican to declare a
statement of Pope John Paul II infallible. That was when he
stated that the issue of the ordination of women was decided for
all time, that the church had no authority to ordain women, and
the issue could not be discussed any further. However, that statement was not accepted by the church generally, and the Vatican,
as far as I am aware, no longer claim it to be an infallible statement.

I know this question of infallibility is a delicate topic in today's
church. I think I am right in stating that it was the final straw
that fractured the relationship between the Vatican and Hans
Kung. But it does urgently need to be clarified, both at a theological level, and maybe even more so, at the level of the ordinary
faithful. The line Bernard Haring took in his last book, My Hope
for the Church, written shortly before he died, if I understand it
correctly, makes sense to me. Infallibility, and by definition infallible pronouncements, can only happen when there is a genuine

openness on all sides in the church. It involves a reciprocal relationship between the pope and church members. The pope needs
to have listened carefully to the church at large, to bishops, theologians and the faithful. The word Haring uses is 'received'. The
pope needs to be seen to have received the opinion of the church.
And then, when the pope has pronounced on the particular topic,
the pronouncement, in turn, needs to be received by the faithful.
If either of those conditions is not present, then infallibility is impossible. In this context it is interesting to look at the encyclical
of Paul VI on contraception, *Humanae Vitae*. Vatican spokesmen
at the time tried to elevate that to the status of infallibility. But,
in the understanding of Haring, it clearly failed on both counts.
The pope did not 'receive' the view of the large majority of the
commission he himself had set up to study the topic. And then a
substantial amount of the Catholic faithful did not 'receive' the
teaching, when it was promulgated. The same can be said for the
teaching on the ordination of women. In fact, if Haring's definition of infallibility is accurate, I think it is fair to say that in the
present church, where there is little or no real discussion or consultation possible, the conditions for any form of infallible statement are not present.

Another aspect of the question of papal primacy and infallibility which has enormous implications is the effect these two
doctrines have on our relationship with other Christian churches.
There is no doubt that the intense desire for supremacy shown by
the papacy of the Roman church was one of the major reasons for
the original split with the eastern churches. And the problem of
papal infallibility has been a significant stumbling block in dialogue with other Christian churches in the west.

I think it was a big mistake to ever declare the pope infallible,
and that it was done for fairly questionable motives. But now that
we have it, maybe we can at least clarify it in a way that makes
sense to people.

As a footnote to what I have just said, I think it is worth high-lighting the tragedy for the church of the tension between the authorities and the theologians for the past thirty years. It is not the first time this has happened. Pope Pius XII, in the 1950s, placed many of the best theologians of his time under various forms of censure. The era of the Second Vatican Council, in contrast, was notable for the close cooperation between theologians and bish-ops. The division became evident again after *Humanae Vitae*, and it was accentuated during the pontificate of Pope John Paul II. It is unfortunate for both sides. The quality of statements coming from the authorities has suffered from the lack of good theologi-cal background, and probably even more so from a good scriptural basis. The theologians, for their part, have too often got one eye fixed on the Vatican and the possible reaction there when they are writing their articles and books.

Appointment of Bishops

There needs to be a serious look taken at the whole system of appointing bishops in the church. For most of the history of the church the pope didn't have the right to appoint bishops every-where in the church. In many places bishops were elected. But one of the historical problems the church had was the interfer-ence of the local civil leaders. They wanted to have a say in the appointment of the bishop. In the more extreme cases they man-aged to appoint one of their own families as bishop. This is partly the reason why Rome took all the appointments to itself. But that danger is no longer present in the church, except in some excep-tional cases.

The present system has two weaknesses, as I see it. Firstly, the fact that Rome appoints all bishops means a centralising of power, with no say for the local church. To quote Haring, again from his last book, *My Hope for the Church*:

Every misguided appointment of a bishop by Rome reflects badly on the prestige of the papacy and harms the trusting relations between Rome and the local churches.

We have seen many examples of this in recent times. If we look, for instance, at the bishops chosen in Irish dioceses for the past twenty years or so; how many of them would have been chosen by the local church? Very few, I suspect.

The second problem with the system is that a particular administration in Rome has the power to appoint its friends and fellow-travellers to all the positions of influence, bishoprics and theological faculties. I believe this has been a feature of recent administrations in the church. It is surely unhealthy when only one point of view is allowed to be heard in an organisation. Why, we must ask, is the Vatican so concerned with holding on to power? Again, from Haring:

> There is no avoiding the fact: behind all efforts at centralisation lies a lack of trust that the Spirit of God wishes to work in and through everyone.

In this, as in many other ways, the centralised apparatus of power reinforced under the long pontificate of Pope John Paul II is destructive of the good of the church.

Decision-making in the Church

More church members need to be involved in the process of decision-making. At the moment it is confined to a group of elderly male celibates. There is nothing wrong with being elderly, male or celibate. But an authority system that is vested exclusively in people who are all three is clearly deficient, because it excludes so many others. This is such an obvious point that I find it hard to see how the church continues with such a defective form of government. Most of the people who have the real authority

within the church are long past the age when they would have retired in any other institution. I am not suggesting that older people have nothing to offer, and I think the modern world has gone
to the other extreme in putting too much emphasis on youth, and
often throwing people on the scrap-heap when they reach middle
age. But if the only people with power are old, then there is clearly
a problem. Watching the church elders (an appropriate title!) gather in the Vatican, as they did for the recent funeral and conclave, always brings to my mind the pictures of the Chinese leadership under Mao. It is an unfortunate similarity.

Council of Bishops

I think it is both possible and necessary to resurrect the idea of a
council of bishops, as was attempted during the Second Vatican
Council. This is an essential idea, and would be a starting point
in the spreading out of decision-making. If an effective council of
bishops could be put in place it would help to rid us of the curse
of centralisation. The voices of all the different churches around
the world would be heard, and would be part of decision-making.
It would be essential then to move on from there and allow the
voices of lay people to be heard also. This would radically change
the way the church operates, and would imbue new life and
energy into it at all levels. It would have great and exciting implications for ecumenism. What we are dealing with here is a simple principle. Do we believe that the Spirit is with all the believers, or only with bishops, cardinals and popes? If we believe God
speaks through the whole community of believers, then there is
no longer any valid reason for continuing with the present system.

I think there is a certain arrogance in the Catholic church
when it comes to creating structures which allow for more people
to be involved in decision-making. Very often I hear the comment made that if we go down that road we will be following in

the footsteps of the Protestants (in our context that usually means Anglicans), and the assumption is that they are in a bad state, and we have nothing to learn from them. A bit more humility on our part would be helpful. We can actually learn a great deal from the Anglicans, as from other Christian churches.

I will leave the last words on the topic to Bernard Haring. After a long life lived in complete dedication to the church, and in close proximity to the Vatican, he had this to say:

> The Roman Curial system has to be downsized. We could do without cardinals altogether. The pope himself should not appoint the men who will choose his successor. The powers and responsibilities of the conferences of bishops and their regional assemblies have to be enhanced. The election of the pope has to be internationally representative, with women participating.

Can any of this happen? I believe so. And I also believe that it is crucial for the future of the church that changes are made.

III

THE SUPPRESSION OF IDEAS

In the history of the Catholic church the period from the Protestant Reformation to the middle of the twentieth century, and specifically the Second Vatican Council, was by any standards an extraordinarily introverted period. It is worth looking at because of the way it has influenced our time and all that has happened within the church in the past fifty years. When I say that the church had become introverted I mean that it had turned in on itself, adopting a defensive, and even dogmatic, attitude towards the world at large. The Second Vatican Council brought that era to an end, and tried to initiate a big change in thinking within the church, and especially in the relationship between the church and the world. Pope John XXIII tried to reorientate the church, towards the world rather than away from it, in dialogue with the world rather than antagonistic to it. Unfortunately in the last twenty years or so the church has tended to lose its nerve and revert back to the pre-council attitudes.

Aftermath of the Protestant Reformation
The struggle that followed the Protestant Reformation in the sixteenth century, and the way the church reacted to the reformers, set the scene for the following four centuries. The leadership of the church at the time reacted very negatively and aggressively towards the reformers. In hindsight this was a great pity. If they had the ability, or maybe the confidence in themselves and in what they believed, to listen to and take seriously what the reformers

were saying, to consider what areas of church life might actually be in need of reforming, the course of world history could have been changed. But they didn't, and their antagonistic position was solidified and institutionalised by the Council of Trent (1545), at which a lot of church teaching was promulgated in a tone and content that was adversarial to say the least. I believe the church has suffered greatly as a consequence. We see once again the problem of a church that believes it possesses the whole truth. It was incapable of recognising that there might be some justification to what the reformers were saying. For the church leadership there was only one attitude to be adopted; the reformers were in error, and the only way they could be free from their error was to return to the fold of the church, and renounce their false teachings. Humility has never been a strong point with the church; the tendency has always been to proclaim the truth from a superior position rather than to listen and learn. Believing that you possess the whole truth is probably the most dangerous belief of all. It promotes arrogance, an unhealthy sense of superiority, and a narrow judgemental response to anything outside its own circle. It is out of this mentality that the church, for the next 400 years, largely rejected the world around it, took up a position of condemnation towards it, and was slow to the point of nearly being incapable of learning from the world, or from anybody outside the narrow confines of the church.

A Church out of Touch with the World

In the meantime life carried on, as life tends to do. Even during its most powerful and autocratic times the church hasn't been able to put a halt to the development and progression of humanity, and of human thought. Momentous events and movements took place during those centuries. The French Revolution at the end of the eighteenth century was probably one of the most cataclysmic events in the history of humanity, and its ripples are being felt to this day. It was followed by the Enlightenment period, which introduced new ways of thinking and behaving. The nineteenth century saw the development of industrialisation, which brought enormous changes, for good and ill, into the lives of ordinary people. During all this time the church largely remained untouched and unchanged, neither influencing nor being influenced by what was going on around it. This was not only true in relation to the Vatican and the papacy. Unfortunately it was also true of the ordinary Catholic. Religious practice had become very devotional, being manifested in devotion to the saints expressed in novenas and similar exercises, and, from the middle of the nineteenth century on, a big upsurge in devotion to Mary. In itself there was nothing wrong with any of that, but when it was combined with the fact that there was little theological reflection going on, it certainly constituted a problem. Religious practice was based more on emotion than on intellect and reason. There is of course place for both. But a balance needs to be kept, and in the nineteenth and early twentieth centuries the balance tipped too much in favour of emotional responses without the guidance of reason. In some places, France for instance, social action movements were founded and began to do good work among the poor in the cities during the industrial revolution. While this was a true expression of Christianity, the type of radical thinking about the structures of church or society which might have accompanied it did not happen. Church life mainly ran on a different track to the world, and they tended not to meet. Hans Kung sums it up as follows in his historical work, *Christianity; the Religious Situation of our Time*:

> A closed mind, submission, humility and obedience to an increasingly narrow-minded and arrogant hierarchy were regarded as central to Catholic virtues.

The Worker Priest Movement

As the twentieth century advanced it became increasingly difficult for the church to maintain this attitude of aloofness. Influences from outside were beginning to change the thinking of
theologians, and even more so of priests and nuns working at the
coal face of life. As always, some people were ahead of their time,
acting as agents of change, and in other instances necessity was
becoming the mother of invention. The Second Vatican Council
did not come out of the blue. The movement of thought and action had begun some years earlier. A good example of this was the
worker priest movement in France after the Second World War.
This was an interesting development. The bishops of France became alarmed at the fact that only two per cent of the labour
force of the country was going to Sunday mass. Led by the cardinal archbishop of Paris, Emmanuel Suhard, they initiated a movement of the church reaching out to the workers. A number of
priests took jobs in factories. The idea was that they would mix
with the people at a very ordinary day-to-day level, as one of their
own, and in this way attempt to introduce some aspects of Christian faith into their lives. It was a daring and innovative idea. But
it quickly raised many questions that made the church authorities
in Rome very nervous, questions about ministry, the feasibility of
part-time priests, compulsory celibacy, subjects that were not open
for discussion in the church. The worker priests inevitably became drawn into the struggle for better wages and conditions for
their fellow workers. Because many of the priests were well educated they began to be elected to position in the unions, unions
that were strongly socialist, even communist, in their philosophy.
The official church was terrified of the influence of communism,
and church leaders were afraid that the worker priests, instead of
bringing Christianity to the workplace, would themselves become sympathetic to communist ways of thinking. So by 1953
Rome had decided to bring an end to the experiment. They de-

creed that the priests return to their parishes and monasteries, and this tentative effort at devising a new style of ministry to meet a particular need ended. In all there had only been ninety worker priests. It was a small experiment, in the context of a total priestly population in France at the time of about 50,000. But it had caught the imagination of the world, and been widely reported in the media. Hans Kung commented:

> The end of the worker priests was a tragedy. And the end of the worker priests was also the end of the theology which supported them.

Here he was referring to a theology that promoted a positive attitude towards the world, and emphasised the centrality of social justice in Christian teaching. That same theology re-emerged some thirty years later in South America in the form of what became known as liberation theology. The reaction of the church authorities was similar. Liberation theology, and its main proponents, was suppressed.

Of the ninety worker priests forty did not return to their priestly duties. They disappeared from history. Their story has never been told. The church once again withdrew into itself, and turned its back on the world. But not for much longer.

A Maelstrom of Ideas
Methods of communication were improving, television and radio had made the world a smaller place, and it was becoming harder and harder to keep people insulated from the maelstrom of ideas that was going on outside the church. I was in the seminary in the 1960s. The Vatican Council was in progress, and the beginnings of change were happening in the liturgy. But by and large the system of seminary training continued on as it had done for centuries. Yet my memory is of a large group of young men, living a very enclosed life but alive with the ideas and attitudes of our

time. Modern literature of all types was being avidly read and discussed. I was particularly fascinated by the books of Simone de Beauvoir, a French writer, partner and lover of Jean Paul Sartre, one of the leading thinkers in the philosophical movement known as Existentialism. She was an atheist, and about the most unlikely person that one would think a young student for the Catholic priesthood should be reading. Yet this sort of thing was common at the time. It showed that the church's very successful 400 year policy of blocking out 'alien' ideas was no longer working. Myself and another student called Paddy were particularly taken by de Beauvoir's autobiographical account, *Memoirs of a Dutiful Daughter*. It is difficult to go back almost forty years to discover what exactly our frame of mind was at that time. What was it that attracted us to Simone de Beauvoir? There is no doubt she was a good writer, and in her memoirs she told her story in a fresh, readable way. It was the character Zaza that most appealed to us. Zaza was Simone's closest school friend. She was from a very traditional Catholic background and the book recounts her struggle to break free from an oppressive and claustrophobic upbringing. She ultimately failed, dying in her early twenties:

> The doctors called it meningitis, encephalitis; no one was quite sure. Had it been a contagious disease, or an accident? Or had Zaza succumbed to exhaustion and anxiety? She has often appeared to me at night, her face all yellow under a pink sun-bonnet, and seeming to gaze reproachfully at me. We had fought together against the revolting fate that had lain ahead of us, and for a long time I believed that I had paid for my own freedom with her death.

Looking back now I wonder if at some level Paddy and myself were revolting against the fate that lay ahead of us, and did we too see ourselves as victims of an oppressive and claustrophobic background that guided us to where we were. I don't know. Paddy died in a tragic accident as a young priest in Brazil, long before he would have had time to work out the answers to complex questions like these. For me the freedom of thought displayed by de Beauvoir left its mark. She had broken away from her background and, through reading and study, had developed a new way of thinking and behaving. I found her exciting and exhilarating. We sat for hours in one or other of our smoke-filled rooms (the dangers of passive, or indeed active, smoking had not impacted on our consciousness yet – and anyway we were young and were going to live forever!) and discussed the ideas of de Beauvoir. We saw ourselves as sharing her rebelliousness, her rejection of authority in all its guises. We were probably not aware that de Beauvoir had been listed in the index of books forbidden to Catholics. Even if we had we would have laughed at the idea of such an index, and it wouldn't have worried us because we believed that the Second Vatican Council had changed everything. Rebelliousness, rejection of the authoritarianism of the past, had now become respectable. The future was ours. We would overcome! Definitely things had changed. The church was no longer closed off and isolated from the world. But we were too young to realise how naïve our views were, and what a doughty opponent the traditional church would prove to be.

The Syllabus of Errors

Two classic examples of the Catholic church's rejection of the modern world were the syllabus of errors and the index of books forbidden to Catholics. These were introduced during the pontificate of Pius IX in the nineteenth century. This was the same pope who summoned the First Vatican Council, and who was responsible for introducing the doctrine of papal infallibility, which I have mentioned in the previous chapter. He intensified the church's rejection of the world, which had been going on since the Reformation. The syllabus of errors was introduced in 1864. It was a list of ideas that were classified as erroneous or wrong. In this he listed many of the new ideas of the Enlightenment period. One of his main targets in this syllabus of errors was the Declaration of the Rights of Man and the Citizen, which originated with the French revolutionaries in 1789, and is probably its greatest legacy. True, the revolution itself, as it progressed, deviated seriously from the ideals of the declaration. But this does not take away from the force and significance of the document, and the influence it has had down to our own time.

It is worth quoting a few of these declarations:

Men are born and remain free and equal in rights.
- The aim of every political association is the preservation of the natural and inviolable rights of man. These rights are liberty, property, safety and resistance to oppression.
- Liberty consists of being able to do anything which is not harmful to another person.
- No one shall be harassed for his opinions, even religious opinions, provided they do not disturb public order as established by law.
- Freedom of thought and expression is one of the most precious rights of man.

Read from a modern perspective this declaration does not appear particularly striking. But coming out of the age in which it was written, it was truly revolutionary. To a world still familiar with the concept of slavery, and where social and political divisions were deeply set and unchanging, to assert that every human being was equal in rights was truly remarkable.

Three ideas stand out clearly here:

- That every human person is born free, and is entitled to freedom.
- That every person has the right to freedom of thought and expression.
- That freedom of conscience, freedom to practise whatever

religion one chooses as long as it does not interfere with
others, is also an inalienable right.

It is a sobering thought that a pope in the nineteenth century,
and one that the church later declared to be a canonised saint, was
such a vehement opponent of these ideas that he declared them
anathema, and not to be entertained by any Catholic. They are
such obvious Christian ideas, so clearly in tune with the teaching
of the Gospel. Jesus stressed the incalculable value of every human person ('every hair on your head is counted'; 'you are of
more value than many sparrows'), and the importance of freedom
('the truth will set you free'). Instead of being in the forefront of
the promotion of these ideas, the pope and the church strongly
opposed them.

All of this is indicative of how far the popes and bishops of
that time had deviated from the Gospel message. They had modelled themselves on the mediaeval kings and emperors, who believed themselves to be divinely appointed, and ruled by decree.
And, like any mediaeval ruler, they wanted to keep all their people in submission. Ideas like freedom of thought or speech were
threatening to their power and position. So they fought against
them in every way they could. Freedom of conscience, the belief
that every person should be free to believe and practise what they
chose, as long as it did not interfere with the rights of others, was
totally alien to them. A church that regarded itself as the sole
custodian of the truth inevitably had difficulty in seeing the value
of freedom of conscience. Agree with us and you will be saved;
disagree and you will be damned. Not much room for either freedom of thought or conscience there. It was an arrogant church,
but paradoxically one that was also very frightened, full of fear
that these new ideas might threaten its power and prestige. It is
ironic that during the nineteenth century the non-Catholics, and
maybe even more so the non-believers, were the ones who most

promoted these fundamental aspects of the Christian message.

In all the syllabus of errors contained a list of eighty ideas that were condemned. Hans Kung sums up the attitude of the official church:

> Human rights generally were condemned: freedom of conscience, religion and the press, and civil marriage. So too were naturalism, rationalism, socialism and communism, and any rejection of the Papal States.

They were all false, and to be condemned. It is hard to imagine the mentality at work in the church at this time. There was the sheer arrogance of the pope in setting himself up as a judge of the great minds, and some of the great movements, of his time, and seeming to dismiss them with such certainty. He was convinced he was right, that he could do no wrong, could not make a mistake.

For a century or more Pius IX and his successors appeared to be successful. Through a vigorous exercise of centralised authority, and strict discipline, they managed to create a cocoon around the church, which effectively isolated it from the world outside, and all the dramatic changes that were happening.

What can be said about the church of those centuries? It must have been a very insecure church. It seemed to feel un-der threat from everything that was outside of itself, that was new or different. How did the church become like that? Maybe it was part of the legacy of the Reformation, that period when it lost so many of its adherents, and was now fearful of losing more. What really stands out is that the church modelled itself on secular power, and not on the message of Jesus whose kingdom was not of this world. Neither did it inherit the fear and insecurity from Jesus. There is none of that in his teaching. He put his message out strongly and clearly, and challenged the accepted values and beliefs of his time, but he in no way tried to coerce anyone into belief. Nor did he act as if his message was weak and inadequate, and could not cope with alternative ways of looking at things. He didn't cut himself off from his generation; he was a man of his time, well acquainted with the beliefs and lifestyle of his contemporaries. He wasn't afraid to criticise or critique anything that he disapproved of, and to praise what he saw as good. He was of his age. It is hard to escape the conclusion that the post-reformation Catholic church was no longer a proper vehicle for the teaching of Christ. I think it is clear why, when the church today claims to have been founded by Christ and to be exactly as Christ wished it to be, many of us are slow to accept it. Many times down through history the church deviated widely from what Christ would have wished, and I have no doubt that it continues to do so today.

The Index of Books Forbidden to Catholics

The other classic sign of church insecurity and fear on the one hand, and its desperate effort to control the minds of its followers on the other, was the index of books forbidden to Catholics. This index really is extraordinary, and younger people today would find it very hard to understand the mentality behind it. Those of us who grew up in the Ireland of the middle of the last century understand it well; we had a similar level of state censorship in those times. Between what was forbidden by the church and the state there was a lot we were not supposed to read.

The index reads almost like a who's who of the great writers of the nineteenth and first half of the twentieth centuries. Descartes and Pascal are just some of the philosophers listed; the British empiricists Hobbes, Locke and Hume, and of course Kant; John Stuart Mills and the historian Gibbons. Many of the great writers and thinkers of the early twentieth century are also listed: Victor Hugo, Alexander Dumas, Balzac, Zola, Jean-Paul Sartre, Simone de Beauvoir, and, nearer our own time, Gide and Kazantzakis, the man who gave us Zorba the Greek. Not only were these writers of distinction; they were also some of the great thinkers, some of the people who most shaped the intellectual life of the twentieth century.

Here again, as with the syllabus of errors, the church showed what a fearful organisation it was. If Catholic people read these books they might be introduced to new ways of looking at things, they might no longer be docile and easy to teach. It was also a very patronising church. The church leaders clearly looked on the ordinary Catholic as being simple, uneducated and easily led, people whose thinking had to be done for them. It ignored the fact that every human person has a mind of their own, and it was insulting to treat them in this way. It was also insulting to the faith. If it was so weak that it could not stand up to argument and alternative points of view, then it would be useless. Authoritarianism had taken over, and the result is explained well by Peter C. Morea in his book, *Towards a Liberal Catholicism*:

> In an authoritarian organisation, personal conscience is subordinated to authority. In the authoritarian tradition, fear is regarded as a legitimate means of enforcing obedience; a religious authoritarianism not only wishes to subordinate to its authority people's behaviour but also what they think and feel.

Hans Kung had this to say about that era:

> All this confirms impressively how far Rome had gone on the defensive with the mediaeval Roman Catholic paradigm. For the modern world had largely come into being without and against Rome and moreover went its way, not at all impressed by the backward-looking utopia of a Papal State bureaucracy dreaming of the Middle Ages and hostile to the Reformation and to reform generally. Hardly any attempt was made to engage in a critical constructive discussion with modern atheism.

Suppression of Scholarship

The result of all of this was that the church had largely opted out of the intellectual debate for hundreds of years. That went hand in hand with an almost complete suppression of scholarship within the church itself. The seminary course that was taught in the 1950s had hardly changed at all in 300 years. It was certainly not influenced by the Enlightenment, the great revolutions, or the world wars. The amazing project of the Vatican, cutting the church off from the world, was similar to what was attempted, though much less successfully, by the Communist bloc. The communists built walls and high fences around their borders. They did not let their people out, and attempted to prevent any influences from outside coming in. Theirs was a physical border. The church on the other hand set up an intellectual and spiritual border. It told people that new ideas would endanger the salvation of their souls. Both realised the power of a new idea, and how, if it was let loose, it could not be restrained again. Right down to the 1950s the church continued to act in this way. Pope Pius XII, who was pope until 1959, was still silencing and removing theologians from office all over Europe. These theologians were generally removed without any explanation or appeal. In many cases it meant also depriving them of their livelihood. No question of human rights here! In the early 1950s he removed from office a large number of Jesuits, the best known being Henri de Lubac. Then in 1954, after the suppression of the worker priest movement, three provincials and a number of theologians belonging to the French Dominicans were removed. Probably the greatest example was the silencing of Yves Congar, who was generally recognised as the outstanding Catholic theologian of the time. Hans Kung, in *My Struggle for Freedom*, describes how, as a student in Rome, he met Congar during the time he was silenced. His comment makes for sad and sombre reading:

Congar deeply abhorred the system [the Vatican], which he compared with that of Stalin [and the 'Holy Office' with the Gestapo], because with denunciation and secrecy it creates an atmosphere of suspicion and rumours in the church, and is ultimately based on fear, fear not only of communism but of any change to the status quo.

Kung is right that fear was a big factor in influencing the church to behave as it did during that time. But it was also a desperate effort to cling to power, and to the high degree of control that it had exercised over the Catholic world and over the individual lives of Catholic people. In its closed, narrow mentality it had completely lost the spirit of St Paul, who was willing to engage with the Greek philosophers, the pagans, and all the different beliefs of his time. He was confident of the power of the message he had received.

So when we hear the phrase attributed to Pope John XXIII, about opening the windows and letting the breeze in, we can see what he meant. There were hundreds of years of stagnant air to be blown away. The corridors of power in the Vatican were littered with the cobwebs of fear, of stagnation, of centuries of effort to keep people in compliant ignorance. It is no surprise that the fresh air of change, the unsettling anarchy of new ideas, did not receive a total welcome among the inhabitants of that institution. They must have been seriously threatened by it. Change was not going to come easily.

Liberation

When I read up and think on this long period in the church's history I am reminded of Bernard Haring's sentence: 'Liberation is absolutely unthinkable without freedom of speech'.

For centuries the church had done everything it could to prevent freedom of speech, to silence dissent. It had used shameless and destructive means to achieve this. The inquisition stands out for its cruelty and evil. It is hard to understand how cardinals,

bishops and even popes, justified the torture and killing of people
who disagreed with them. But in fact they did this for a long
period of the church's history. Later, when they no longer had the
power to put people to death, they used other methods to silence
them and remove them from office. So, if Haring is correct, then
for those centuries there has been little enough liberation in the
Catholic church. I'm sure most people will agree that liberation
is a central Christian idea; 'The truth will set you free', Jesus said.
That marvellous story in John's Gospel which describes the raising of Lazarus contains a great sentence. Like all the stories in
John's Gospel, it is written from a theological rather than a historical point of view. The story is told in such a way as to carry
deep meaning about the person and message of Jesus. So, after Lazarus comes out of the tomb, and when Jesus turns to the onlookers
and says 'Unbind him and let him go free', we are meant to read
that sentence as a statement about his whole ministry, and ad-
dressed not just to Lazarus but to all of us. He has come to set us
free, to remove the shackles that are binding us, holding us back
from being the people we are capable of becoming. The message
of Jesus is a message of freedom. There is no way that his life and
teaching can justifiably be used to support a church that tries to
keep its followers in ignorance and bondage. The only conclusion
we can come to is that the church had lost sight of the reason and
purpose of its existence – spreading the message of Christ.

The Years after the Second Vatican Council
By the beginning of the 1960s there was clearly a big problem;
the church was in urgent need of change and reform. This was
the aim of Pope John XXIII when he convened the Second Vatican Council. He was successful up to a point. After years of being
closed and inward-looking, the church opened itself up both to
the other Christian churches and to the world in general. The
document 'Gaudium et Spes, The Church in the Modern World'

has a completely different view of the world to the traditional official church one. In future the attitude of the church to the progress of humanity is to be in principle positive, though not uncritical. It declares itself to be in solidarity with humanity. It is challenged to recognise the signs of the times, and to interpret them in the light of the Gospel. It is on the side of human dignity, freedom, the rights of the person, and the development and improvement of human society. This is an enormous change.

But the years after the council have not lived up to the many promises that came out of that event. Hans Kung, in My *Struggle for Freedom*, gives a fascinating account of the intense power struggle that went on during the years of the council between the Curia and the bishops. As I described in the previous chapter, he tells how the Curia came out triumphant, largely because Pope Paul VI chose not to challenge and break its power. Bernard Haring played a significant part in the council as a theological adviser, and lived in Rome for most of the rest of his life. He had an intimate view of the Vatican at work. He describes the concerted efforts made to return to the pre-council days of repression. The papacy now sought to control the theologians. He saw the pontificate of Pope John Paul II as marked by a whole series of measures aimed at cutting off all reactions, except positive ones, to papal pronouncements:

> Theologians, especially moralists, have again and again been admonished to make the pope's statements the strict guideline for all their efforts. The chief, if not the only, concern here is sexual ethics, on which the pope has had a great deal to say. Today we have to confront the attempt by another restoration to achieve absolute conformity with all papal teaching through sanctions against nonconformists. This quest for conformity is being carried out in conjunction with a previously unheard-of exercise of power by means of the appointment of bishops and the strictest oversight in filling theological chairs and other church offices.

In other words, the mentality of the previous centuries has once again come to dominate. The open dialogue with the other Christian churches and with the world has been drastically curtailed. Alternative opinions, labelled as dissent, in all their forms have been rejected. As in earlier times, creative theologians like Leonardo Boff have been silenced and removed from their posts. Total control has been exercised over all church appointments. Uniformity is imposed wherever possible. A major effort is being made to close those windows that Pope John XXIII opened, and to dispel that disturbing and liberating fresh air he let in. Theology has stagnated, because too many theologians are looking over their shoulder in order to avoid antagonising the Vatican authorities. Bishops are submissive, and mostly exercise their submissiveness by silence. They are caught in an impossible position, between the demand for uniformity of thinking and behaviour on the one hand, and a very diverse and challenging world on the other. Fear and insecurity are again a feature of church life.

I will quote from Morris West:

> In a very strange way, it seems to me that the role of authority within the church has been distorted. The exercise of authority is not, and cannot be, a self-determining, self-sufficing act like the act of creation. The only justification of the *magisterium* is as a function of *ministerium*, of service to souls who are the subjects and objects of salvation. To use a very ancient and primitive symbol, we are not the makers of fire; we are the carriers of fire for the tribe which does not know how to make it. On too many occasions in history, the keepers of fire have turned into tyrants or cold-hearted conservators of that which they do not own.

The fire that we are carrying is the wonderful, liberating message of Jesus Christ, who came to give us life. If we distort and diminish the message, we are selling out on the future generations in an unforgivable way.

But it is now the twenty-first century. The effort to restore the past cannot succeed. People are more educated, communication is easy, and ideas can no longer be locked away.

Either the church once again puts the liberation of humanity at the centre of its message and its practice or it will become increasingly marginalised and irrelevant.

On 7 February 1600 a man called Giordano Bruno was burned for heresy in Rome, one of the many victims of the Inquisition. Morris West wrote a play about him, called *The Heretic*. Commenting on the play, in his book, *A View from the Ridge*, he said the following:

> One of the men who signed the monstrous document of Bruno's condemnation was Cardinal Robert Bellarmine, a canonised saint, known to his contemporaries as the meekest of men. How could he do it? I have thought often about this. I have come to the conclusion that institutional power distances men and women from their own humanity. They forget that men and women are the subjects and objects of salvation, not institutions.

I have chosen that quote to sum up this chapter. It is a chapter about an institution that became obsessed with its own survival and as a consequence failed to show sufficient concern for the salvation of humanity, which is the only possible purpose of its existence, an institution driven by fear and using fear as a method of control. Only a few fragments remain of the record of Bruno's trial. But we do know his final words, after sentence was passed on him:

> At this moment, gentlemen, I think that you are more afraid of me than I am of you.

Peter C. Morea explains the psychology of how this can happen to people like Robert Bellarmine, and so many in positions of

authority in the church in recent years who covered up the activities of paedophiles:

> A young Catholic, feeling called by Christ to serve others and particularly the vulnerable, enters a seminary to become a priest. In the years that follow, as curate and parish priest and finally as a bishop, he is surrounded and influenced by fellow-members of the Catholic church. He eventually internalises the view of those around him, that what matters above all is the church, since only if the institution remains strong can the church serve others. His self has become so identified with the organisation that the church's survival and growth is now seen by him as paramount. Without realising, his original reason for entering the priesthood, which was the service of others, has become secondary to the survival and prestige of the organisation.

This quote explains very well how what we call clericalism works, how the male celibates who run the church have become a caste, a closed group who are not capable of listening or learning from outside themselves.

In their book, *The Inquisition*, Michael Baigent and Richard Leigh describe the then Cardinal Joseph Ratzinger, the prefect of the Congregation for the Doctrine of the Faith, and now the pope, as the grand inquisitor of today. Though they go on to say that unlike Dostoevsky's grand inquisitor, Ratzinger is no world-weary cynic. On the contrary there is no reason to doubt his sincerity. They have this to say about him:

> Ratzinger is authentically and profoundly concerned about the current and future affairs of the church. He is anxious to avert a number of crises – of faith, of trust in dogma, of morality – by which he sees the modern church beleaguered. He believes the church must be spared such awkwardness. By existing in a lofty and rarefied sphere of its own, the church should be immune and insulated from the taint and controversy of 'merely' human institutions. For Ratzinger the church is quite literally the 'mystical body of Christ'. He dis-

misses any suggestion that it might ultimately be man-made. On the contrary, the church's fundamental structures are willed by God himself, and therefore they are inviolable. Behind the human exterior stands the mystery of a more than human reality, in which reformers, sociologists, organisers have no authority whatsoever.

We clearly have a great and enormous challenge facing us in the church. Hundreds of years of serving the institution rather than the message have left a legacy of repression and fear. The question that must be asked is a difficult one. Is it possible for our church to once again become the servant and the agent of Christianity rather than of itself?

IV

WOMEN IN THE CHURCH

In this chapter I am going to look at the place of women in the Catholic church. 'What place?' you might justifiably ask, because at the level of authority and decision-making there is little or no place for women in the church. And yet if you examine any congregation at a weekend mass in most churches in the western world, you will find that the large majority are women. It would appear that women are by nature more religious than men, or at least they are more inclined to express their religious beliefs in public than men. It is also true that the majority of the menial tasks in any church building are done by women. They sweep the floor, polish the furniture, look after the candles in front of the shrines, and usually, now that they are allowed into the sanctuary, they prepare the altar for mass. It is true that, in recent years, they act as readers and ministers of the Eucharist. And yet when it comes to deciding about what happens in the church, the nature of the liturgy, the content of the sermons, women have no say. True, in some parishes there are liturgy groups, and women can be members of these groups, so a little progress is happening in this area. But groups like the liturgy group and the pastoral council are totally dependant on the good will of the priest for their existence and for the degree of influence they may have on parish activities. Sometimes a particular priest has facilitated great involvement of people in his parish ministry, and then he is moved on and replaced by someone who disbands the whole structure and goes back to deciding and doing everything for himself. Unfortunately, when this happens, there is nothing the people can do about it. They are never consulted about the appointment or removal of the priest.

At the higher level of authority and decision-making within the church women are almost totally excluded. When the bishops of a country meet, a woman may occasionally be brought in to address them on some particular area of expertise, but the decisions are made by the men alone. We see pictures of them on television, as they walk the grounds of whatever college or hotel in which they are assembled, and they look so old, so black and so male. It is an image of maleness, of exclusivity, of control and domination, but equally one that betrays a sense of being out of touch with the real world. Half the human race is decidedly outside. They can watch from a distance, see it on their screens, but they cannot be a part of it. This image is even more pronounced when we see a meeting of bishops or cardinals in Rome. This group is even older, more ceremonially dressed in the garb which dates back to the Roman Empire, and even more distant and exclusive. In recent times a small number of women have been appointed to positions in the Vatican that had previously been occupied by men, but I believe it is still true that no senior position of any significance is occupied by a woman. Still we must welcome any small chink in the armour of that male bastion. At an official level there is a very strict line which asserts that women cannot be ordained to the priesthood. But that is usually followed by some conciliatory statement that other offices of significance are open to them. The reality is that they are not. It would be a brave woman that would join the parade of cardinals, even if she was invited! The result is that in an organisation which is largely supported and sustained by women, all the decisions are made by men. This is self-evidently an intolerable situation, one that cannot be sustained. If the Catholic church was a non-religious body it would long ago have been brought to court under equality law along with many other of the major world religions.

Women Begin to Question

The past twenty or thirty years have seen a big change in attitude and thinking about this situation among ordinary Catholics. The change may not have been so pronounced if the meetings of bishops or cardinals continued to be about matters that were removed from the ordinary lives of people. Most people would happily leave them alone, and let them get on with it. But when the church was seen to be making decisions that deeply affected people at a personal level the spotlight began to focus on them more searchingly. This is why I think that the debate and decision on artificial contraception changed the face of the Catholic church. I deal with *Humanae Vitae*, and the circumstances surrounding it, in another part of this book. I think it had a dramatic effect on many women in the church. When the Vatican made a statement which laid down a rigid law on matters to do with their bodies and their most intimate relationships, they began to look in a new way at the people who were making these decisions. They started examining the whole of church teaching on sex and relationships more critically. Women began to realise that it was biased very much in favour of the man. A woman was supposed to have sex whenever her husband wished it, and if she got pregnant she had to accept what she was told was 'the will of God' for her. It was part of her duty towards her husband. When the church approved of what it called natural methods of contraception, and outlawed anything regarded by them as artificial, one of the consequences was that a woman could only have sex when it was 'safe'. The fact that the supposedly safe time was also the time when a woman might be least inclined to have sex was not considered. As these and other issues came to light, women began to ask who were making the decisions. Inevitably they began to question why there wasn't a female voice in there, to represent the reality of their lives. The fact that the decisions were made exclusively by men was bad enough, but the fact that these men were celibate, and presumably more cut off from women than the ordinary man would be, made it worse.

So the *Humanae Vitae* controversy raised the question of women, and their place in the church, in a new way, and the question remains, and will remain until such time as it is faced, and a resolution sought. I have little or no doubt that it is potentially the most explosive issue facing the Catholic church in the immediate future. The struggle and pain that the Anglican and Episcopalian churches had to go through when they decided to allow women be ordained is probably only a small reflection of what it will be like for the Catholic church. We in the Catholic church have traditionally been very slow to accept change, and historically we have tended only to accept things many years after society in general has embraced them. A good example, which I have dealt with earlier in this book, is the way the church condemned human rights and freedom of speech in the nineteenth century, and only very slowly came around to accepting them, long after they had been accepted by the general mass of people, even though as principles they are totally in line with Christian teaching. I presume it will be the same with the issue of the place of women in the church. Eventually the church will be dragged, kicking and screaming, to accepting the equality of women, long after everyone else. But in the meantime, what damage will be done to the faith? How many people, especially women, will have drifted away because they can no longer tolerate what they see as the patronising and domineering attitude of the church?

The Catholic Church and the Importance of Tradition

It is good to look back briefly at this aspect of the history and tradition of the church, to see can we find the origin of some of the attitudes causing problems today. Why is it that the church is so reluctant to dismantle the male bastion it has built up over the centuries, and to allow women equal status? I think there are a number of reasons, which I will try to outline.

One of the points of difference between the Catholic church and other Christian churches is on the question of tradition. I have explained elsewhere that the Catholic church draws its teaching both from the Bible and from tradition, meaning the teaching and knowledge that has built up over the 2,000 year history of the church. Other Christian churches tend to put more emphasis on the Bible, and less, or none at all, on tradition. It is not fully accurate to say that the church has 2,000 years of tradition. In reality it draws on a much longer tradition than that. Because Christianity grew out of the Jewish religion, it has also inherited the thousands of years of belief and practice before the time of Christ, as passed down to us in the Old Testament, and a good deal of those beliefs and customs made their way into Christian belief. There is also another source of tradition which has been influential in the church, namely Greek philosophy. At the time of Christ, and during the early church, the dominant philosophy in that region of the world was Greek. The great Greek philosophers, Socrates, Plato and Aristotle, were by far the most significant influence on the thinking of society at the time, and inevitably they had a major influence on the early church. St Paul was certainly influenced by them, and so were the outstanding scholars of later generations, most notably Augustine and Thomas Aquinas. Not just the church, but the whole way the western world grew and developed was permeated by Greek philosophy.

So the church has inherited an enormous body of tradition, coming from quite diverse sources. It is worth looking at some of this and seeing what type of attitudes to women prevailed in Greek philosophy and in the Old Testament.

A Look at History
The Greek philosopher Aristotle is highly significant because of the way he influenced those who came after him. It is possible to

detect Aristotelian ideas still prevalent 1,500 years after he wrote them down, and indeed even today. He was the great mind of his, and almost any, era. But his attitude to women does not make for good or helpful reading. He didn't exactly have a high opinion of them:

> In terms of nature's own operation, a woman is inferior and a mistake. She is more shameless, lying and deceptive.

He saw woman as a failed man. This idea seems to have developed out of the understanding of the process of procreation that was prevalent at the time. It was believed that the woman had no active part in the creation of new life. Aristotle believed that the male sperm contained the full human being in embryo, and the female body only provided the receptacle in which it grew. If it grew properly and fully it would be male. If there was any defect in it, a female resulted. This is where he got the idea of a woman being a failed man. This seems to have been the crucial point on which centuries of discrimination against women was based. They were seen as only partially developed human beings, and if they had developed properly they would all be men. It is interesting to note that Greek civilisation at the time had great tolerance for homosexual relationships, and in particular relationships between men and boys. I wonder had this anything to do with the very negative attitude to women that prevailed. Whatever about this, there is no doubt that Aristotle had a very significant influence on the early church teachers and preachers. As Garry Wills, the American historian put it in his book, *Papal Sins*:

> Christian teachers and preachers who promulgated these views for more than thirteen hundred years were preaching Aristotle rather than Christ.

All of this is in sharp contrast to the attitude of Jesus. He also lived in a society in which women were seen as inferior beings, but he clearly did not accept this view of them. He treated women as equals in every way, and they were his friends and companions. It is ironic that the great teachers of the early church looked to a Greek philosopher rather than to Christ in order to learn about women and their place in the church.

The Early Church Fathers

I suppose it is somewhat unfair to pick one quote from the body of any person's work, but when it comes to the subject of women some of the more prominent teachers in the early centuries of the church said some fairly colourful things! I will just take four of the early fathers of the church as examples:

> A woman, considering what her nature is, must be ashamed of it. She should cover her head in shame at the thought that she is a woman.
> Clement of Alexandria

Note the influence of Aristotle here. The reason she must be ashamed of her nature is that she isn't a properly developed human being. She is deficient, a failed man. Anybody who believed that would be ashamed of themselves. It is good to remember that at the time there were no female voices to speak out in contradiction to these views. Women were not educated, and were allowed no role in public life.

A slightly different idea comes through in the following quotes:

> Women are the gateway through which the devil comes.
> Tertullian

> Women are easily seduced, weak and lacking in reason. The devil works to spew his chaos out through them.
> Epiphanius, bishop of Cyprus

Women are the gate of hell.

St Jerome

This idea of women as being morally weak and more prone to evil than men is extraordinary. I'm sure it has its origin at least to some extent in the story of the fall of our first parents in the Book of Genesis, and the fact that in the story Eve was the one who first succumbed to temptation. She listened to the persuasion of the devil, appearing to her in the form of a serpent. In all probability this is what Tertullian is referring to when he talks about women as the gateway through which the devil comes. When I was young, growing up in a traditional society in the west of Ireland, the view of women was quite different. Men were regarded as the ones more prone to evil, less responsible and less faithful. It was often said that what a young man needed was a good woman to get him to settle down and be sensible. For many centuries the church, under the influence of Aristotle, thought the opposite.

We can now skip more than a thousand years, and we find that by the thirteenth century things haven't changed very much. One of the great teachers of that era was Albert the Great (I don't think that too many women today would describe him as 'great', if we judge him on this particular attitude):

Woman is a misbegotten man, and has a faulty and defective nature in comparison with his. One must be on guard with every woman, as if she were a poisonous snake and a horned devil.

This quote from Albert the Great is interesting in that it brings together the two ideas prevalent for over a thousand years. Women are failed men, and they are also prone to evil. Aristotle is still alive and well in the writing of Albert. It is worth noting that at this time celibacy had become compulsory for priests. Albert was a celibate. Maybe something of his own personal struggle is reflected in his statement that one must be on guard with every woman. The attractiveness of the woman was a temptation to his vow. Albert the Great was significant in his own right, but probably his greatest significance was that he was a teacher of Thomas Aquinas, who was probably the most influential scholar in the whole history of Christianity. I have mentioned Aquinas elsewhere in this book, and acknowledged that he has made an incalculable contribution to the development of church teaching, but he was not at his best when it came to women and sexuality. Like Albert, it may have had something to do with him being a male celibate living in a monastery, but his genius did not prevent him from having fairly dreadful views on women. To be fair to him he did accept that both man and woman were made in the image and likeness of God, and that was an advance at the time. But he once again echoed Aristotelian views when he said:

> Man is the starting point and goal of woman, and there is something deficient and unsuccessful about woman.

When we gather all of this tradition together (and I only quote from a tiny fraction of it) it amounts to an enormous body of negative views on women from the great teachers of the first 1,300 years of church history. I would have no doubt at all, considering the status the church gives to tradition, that these teachings and attitudes have had a major effect on the thinking of the church right down to our own time. We can see what Gary Wills meant in the quote I used above, about church teachers preaching Aristotle rather than Christ.

The Ordination of Women
If we focus on the ordination of women to the priesthood, probably the most controversial of all the issues concerning women in

the church, we find that it is not a new issue and that the church fathers have interesting things to say:

> Women are not smart enough to be priests.
>
> St John Chrysostom

I remember in the novitiate, the spiritual year for trainee religious, reading the lives of the saints, and one that I was given to read was a life of St John Vianney, the Cure of Ars. It was said about him that he was so academically weak that he was unable to pass any exam, and exceptions needed to be made for him to be ordained to the priesthood. The clear implication of the writer of this particular biography was that St John Vianney was such a wonderful priest and holy man partly because he was simple and decidedly not smart. But the same supposed lack of smartness was considered an insuperable obstacle for women, and no exceptions were made for them.

> Since only the male was made in the image of God, only the male can receive the godlike office of priest.
>
> St Bonaventure

This is not an argument that is still made, at least not overtly, by the church. It was based on a false understanding of the Genesis story about the creation of the world which held that only men were made in the image of God. Now it is fully accepted that it isn't man, as distinct from woman, that is made in the image of God. All human beings are made in the image of God. Traditional societies viewed God as male, since they regarded men as superior. But most people today would accept that God is neither male nor female, or, to put it another way, is as much female as she/he is male. Talking about gender in relation to God really doesn't make sense.

The third interesting quote has an Irish connection. It comes from John Duns Scotus:

> Women, as the successors of Eve, through whom man fell, can-not be the officers of man's salvation.

This one harks back to the notion of women being more prone to evil, made of a weaker moral fibre. It would not be regarded as having any basis in fact today. It is also based on the same false understanding of the Genesis story as the previous quote. Whatever caused evil to come into the world, and led to the downfall of humanity, it surely hadn't to do with women rather than men. It had to do with the tendency towards sin that is in the heart of every human being.

And lastly, Thomas Aquinas, whose view on this was enormously influential:

> Since any supremacy of rank cannot be expressed in the female sex, which has the status of an inferior, that sex cannot receive ordination.

Once more the thinking of Aristotle is being used to justify what is said, that women are inferior. I don't think anybody would dare to use that type of argument any more.

All of the above quotes are from men. During that span of 1,500 years or so from Aristotle to Thomas Aquinas, and indeed for many centuries afterwards, women had little or no say either in society or church. One of the results of all these male views that I have quoted above was that women actually became unequal to men, became inferior in terms of access to power and status. There were a few exceptions. Some women achieved positions of great political power in their countries, like Elizabeth I of England and Isabella of Spain. Paradoxically, the church also provided an opening where women could achieve real positions of importance at a time when society demanded that most women marry and submit to their husbands. Women could enter religious life, and some became abbesses of monasteries, with great influence and power. Theresa of Avila and Catherine of Siena, for example, became both advisers and critics of popes, and in due course were declared doctors of the church.

To suggest that women are inferior to men, or more prone to evil, is completely foreign to us today, because the equality of men and women has become accepted, at least in most cultures in the world. But the church inherited all the negative false views on women, and integrated these views into its sacred tradition. Therefore it shouldn't surprise us that it is still clinging to the notion that women are not eligible to hold any of the ministerial or influential position in its structure. To quote Garry Wills again:

> The long working of poisonous notions – of women's inferiority and impurity – has conditioned our heritage in ways hard to trace and difficult to extrude.

The point he is making, and with which I agree, is that these attitudes, which prevailed for so long in the church, are still the unconscious subtext to many of today's statements and views. Bernard Haring agrees:

> The church as a whole, and the church of Rome in particular, must admit, in shame and repentance, that when it comes to the role and dignity of women it has practically always adhered to the sexism of the time.

In fact it has done worse than that. It has retained sexist attitudes long after society in general had discarded them.

In 1994 Pope John Paul II, in the document 'Sacerdotalis Ordinatio', said:

> I declare that the church has no authority whatsoever to confer priestly ordination on women.

When we hear this we wonder how much Pope John Paul II was speaking out of the terribly flawed and defective tradition we have inherited. I believe it is a major influence. He goes on to try to stifle discussion for all time:

> This judgement is to be definitively held by all the church faithful.

Spokespeople for the Vatican tried to suggest that this statement, and the injunction about having no further discussion on the topic, was infallible. I mention it in the chapter where I deal with the issue of infallibility. The last pope's effort at silencing the church has proved futile. I recently mentioned this ban on discussion to a young female reporter of a television station. She was amazed. The idea of any topic not being available for discussion was completely foreign to her. I could see that the pope was fighting a losing battle on this one. Now he is dead, and the issue continues to be discussed. Thankfully in today's world neither the Vatican nor any other institution can get away with imposing views based on weak and defective arguments on its followers. The issue of women's place in the church will continue to be discussed, and change will inevitably come.

The Jewish Notion of Being Unclean

The other significant influence on Catholic tradition in relation to women is the Old Testament attitude to a woman's monthly cycle. While the Old Testament Jews were in many ways ahead of their time in their views on women, and some women played a significant part in the ancestry of Jesus, yet they had very strange and primitive views on the topic of a woman's menstruation. They believed that a woman, during her monthly period, was ritually unclean. There were many restrictions imposed on her in relation to their religious rituals. For instance, during her days of menstruation she could not enter the inner court of the temple. It is no coincidence that later the church excluded women from the sanctuary, and at one time, even from the church building itself, and the reception of the Eucharist, during menstruation. Jewish priests were not permitted to sleep with their wives on the eve of offering sacrifice. And in later centuries, when priests in the Christian church were still allowed to marry, they too were prohibited from sleeping with their wives before celebrating the Eucharist. The underlying attitude here is clear. Women are unclean, and those who have intimate relations with them also become unclean. Uncleanness in this context is meant in the moral rather than the physical sense. So we can see another source for some of the statements of the church fathers about women being morally weaker and dangerous.

There is a very revealing quote from Pope St Gregory the Great (died 604 AD) about sexual relationships in marriage:

> It is as impossible to have intercourse without sin as it is to fall into a fire and not burn.

There is a story in Matthew's Gospel where a woman with persistent bleeding pushed her way through the crowd and touched the hem of Jesus' cloak. I presume it was included in the Gospel to tell us something about Jesus' attitude to women. The story says she was very afraid. The reason, as I've outlined above, is that in her condition she was considered unclean, and by touching Jesus she would make him unclean also. But clearly Jesus did not believe any of that. He welcomed the woman and healed her.

These attitudes to women that were prevalent in the first millennium of the church's history were the precursors of the declaration of compulsory celibacy for all priests in the twelfth century.

They also add up to a large amount of negative baggage from history. These, along with the attitudes originating with Aristotle,
constitute part of the collective unconscious of today's Catholic
church.

Jesus did not Ordain Anybody

As far as I can judge the main argument used by the church today
against the ordination of women is a simple one. They say that
Jesus did not ordain women, and that as a consequence the church
cannot ordain women either. It is an extraordinary position to
hold. Recently, in response to this argument being used by a senior bishop, a woman wrote a letter to a newspaper in which she
made the point that Jesus did not ordain Irish people either. I felt
it was an appropriate response to the superficiality of the argument that was used.

For a start the argument about Jesus not ordaining women is
weak for the simple reason that most Scripture scholars now accept that Jesus did not ordain anybody to the priesthood. There
is no indication in the teaching of Jesus that he had a ministerial
priesthood in mind. Indeed, as I explained in more detail in an
earlier chapter of this book, it is argued by some scholars that
there is no real indication either that he had a church in mind,
certainly not one like the big institution that developed over the
centuries. Whatever about that, it is undoubtedly true that many
Scripture scholars have already said that Scripture offers no proof
that it is impossible to ordain women. Jesus did choose twelve
apostles, symbolic of the twelve tribes of Israel, and these were all
men, as would be perfectly understandable in the culture in which
he lived. But it is stretching the point to argue that there is a
direct connection between the apostles and today's ministerial
priesthood. It is also worth noting that, according to the Gospel
accounts, women played a significant part in the life and ministry
of Jesus. John's Gospel includes the story of the woman at the

well in Samaria, and depicts her as the first person to whom he revealed that he was the Messiah. She also became probably the first person to preach and proclaim Jesus as the expected one. She went into the village and told all the people about him:

> Come and meet the man who told me everything I have ever done. Could he be the Messiah?

It was also a woman who taught Jesus that his ministry was not just to the Jews, but to the Gentiles as well. Both Mark and Matthew tell the story of the Canaanite woman who appealed to Jesus for help for her daughter who was seriously ill. Jesus told her that he came only for the children of Israel. She persisted, to the point that he insulted her, telling her that it wasn't fair to take the children's food and give it to the house dogs. Even that did not silence her, and in the end he was overwhelmed by her faith and he healed her daughter. In the process she seems to have opened Jesus up to a whole new dimension of his mission. The women were the faithful ones during the passion and death of Jesus; they stayed by the cross and did not run away. And of course it was a woman, Mary of Magdala, who was the first to witness the resurrection and to proclaim it to the other disciples. It seems a strange anomaly that the example of Jesus is now being cited as a reason for declaring that priestly ministry within the church is not open to women.

I outline the development of ministries within the early church elsewhere in this book. I show that there were a variety of ministries in the early Christian communities, and it is notable that many of these ministries were exercised by women. For instance, at the end of the letter to the Colossians, Paul sends best wishes 'to Nympha and the church that meets in her house'.

He is more specific in the letter to the Romans:

I recommend to you our sister Phoebe, who serves the church at
Cenchreae. Receive her in the Lord's name, as God's people should,
and give her any help she may need from you; for she herself has
been a good friend to many people and also to me. I send greetings
to Priscilla and Aquilla [these were husband and wife] my fellow
workers in the service of Christ Jesus, who risked their lives for me.
I am grateful to them – not only I, but all the Gentile churches as
well. Greetings also to the church that meets in their house.

Clearly women were playing a significant part in the ministry of
Paul.

With the advance in our understanding of the Scripture and
the life and ministry of the early church, it is now no longer valid
to call on the practice of Jesus or of the early communities as an
argument against the ordination of women. For the time and the
society in which they lived, both Jesus and the early disciples
were remarkably open in their attitude to women. It was a great
tragedy that the church teachers in the early centuries turned to
Aristotle rather than Christ, and became narrow and discrimina-
tory in their attitudes to women. If instead they had followed the
example of Jesus it would be a very different church today, and nobody would attempt to argue that ordination, or any other ministry within the church, is not possible for women because Jesus did
not ordain women. I find it impossible to believe that Jesus would
be the one who would exclude women from any position, least of
all that of leadership of the Eucharistic assembly.

The other argument used by the church goes something like
this. Jesus was a man, and the priest in celebrating the Eucharist
stands in the place of Jesus and represents him, so he too must be
a man. This is an equally weak argument which seems to me to
hearken back to the views of Augustine about woman being a
failed or a defective man, and as such unable to represent Jesus.
The significance of Jesus is that he came among us as a human
being, not as one particular gender rather than another. When

the priest stands at the altar at mass he doesn't change the bread and wine into the body and blood of Christ. In the name of the community he calls on the Holy Spirit to come and perform the miracle of the Eucharist. Surely it is preposterous to suggest that a man is better able to call on the Holy Spirit than a woman!

Women as Equals in the Church

The argument about women in the church should not be allowed to narrow down to the question of the ordination of women. That is not the only, or indeed the central, issue. What is central is that women should be regarded in the church as equal in every signifi-cant way to men, and that the structure of the church should reflect this belief. Thankfully, some progress is being made. The most dramatic change is in the study of theology. In the western world there are now more women studying theology than men – and this in a profession that was exclusively male up to quite re-cently. Their voice is beginning to be heard and it is certainly a new and fresh voice. In practice, women actually do a lot of minis-tering in the church, particularly in the places where the short-age of vocations to the priesthood is beginning to be felt. Around the world women baptise, preach, lead penitential services, attend to the spiritual needs of the sick and dying, and much more. It is interesting to note that in the Middle Ages abbesses were allowed to hear confession and give absolution in their communities.

So how can the church get itself out of this corner that it has painted itself into, not least our recent popes. This won't happen easily. Any change, while it will be welcomed by the large major-ity of Catholics, will also be stoutly resisted by a hard core of tra-ditionalists. This group had the ear of the Vatican authorities for the duration of the papacy of Pope John Paul II, and the indica-tions are that this situation will continue under the present pope, so realistically it is unlikely that anything will happen in the immediate future.

I think I have made it clear that I believe that there is no real argument to sustain the present position of the church, and I would like to see immediate change, so that all positions in the church would be open to women as much as to men. But I can see that the position outlined by Bernard Haring is probably more realistic, considering the complexity of this issue. He suggests that the church as a whole has first to come to terms with the burden of the past, and, 'in shame and repentance' admit to the awfulness of many of the attitudes of history. Then he calls for the church authorities to exercise patience. Instead of trying to shut off the debate on the one hand, or taking any dramatic decision on the other, they should simply admit that it is a difficult question, with a misfortunate and misguided history. Then allow debate and discussion to proceed at all levels within the church, and trust the Spirit of God to speak through the consensus of the believers. In this way Haring hoped that a resolution would gradually come that would be broadly acceptable and workable.

Whatever way it happens, I see the full inclusion of women in ministry and decision-making as of fundamental importance to the future of the church.

V

SEXUALITY AND HUMAN RELATIONSHIPS

Sex and sexual relationships are at the heart of what it means to be human. Without sexual relationships we would not exist. It is the way designed by the Creator for bringing new life into the world. Sexual identity, and all the desire and passion that go with it, is a major force in all our lives. Coming to terms with our sexuality, learning to be at home in our body with all its desire is one of the big challenges we face in life. In this chapter I am going to write about church attitudes and teaching on sex and the human body.

It is fair to say that the history of the church in this area contains much that is problematic. Historically, we Catholics haven't been particularly at ease with the idea of sex, or the human body. We have tended to be very influenced by the body/soul dichotomy that was prevalent in spirituality for most of the life of the church, a dichotomy that the church resolved by coming down strongly in favour of the soul. The body was seen simply as a vessel for the soul, and of little value in itself. Our real identity was the soul, because it was eternal. The body was mortal; it would die. We weren't beyond going into lurid details about what would happen to it after death, with particular emphasis on the rampaging worms. Some of my ancestors in the Redemptorists specialised in this style of preaching, and could be very colourful on the activities of said worms. What was destined to be the food of worms could hardly be taken seriously.

Creating this division between body and soul, skewed though the attitude was, might not have been too bad, but some of the

Christian teachers went further. The body was to be treated with suspicion, because it was full of dangerous passions and desires that could lead to our destruction, even our damnation. The best thing to do was to discipline and punish it, to keep it strictly under control. Allowing the body to have pleasure became synonymous with sin; taking pride in it was seen as being at odds with Christ's teaching. These attitudes easily became simplified into the notion that the body was evil and the soul good. This created a division at the heart of the human person which was not helpful to mind, body or spirit.

Where did these negative attitudes come from? Can we blame our Jewish origins for them as for some other negative attitudes in Christianity? It would seem not. Take for example the following:

> Your lips are like a scarlet ribbon;
> how lovely they are when you speak.
> Your cheeks glow behind your veil.
> Your neck is like the tower of David,
> round and smooth,
> with a necklace like a thousand shields hung from it.
> Your breasts are like gazelles,
> twin deer feeding among lilies.
> I will stay on the hill of myrrh,
> the hill of incense,
> until the morning breezes blow
> and the darkness disappears.

That certainly doesn't come out of a society or culture that hates the body and all things sexual, quite the opposite. In another place we find the following:

> That you may be suckled, filled,
> from her consoling breasts,
> that you may savour with delight
> her glorious breasts.

SEXUALITY AND HUMAN RELATIONSHIPS

Both of those quotes, of course, are from the Bible: the first one from the Song of Songs, and the second from the Prophet Isaiah, where the writer is using the imagery of human sexuality to illustrate our relationship with God. This tells us that at least some parts of Jewish culture (and Jesus was Jewish) were very much at ease with human love and sexuality. There is absolutely no indication in the teaching of Jesus that he was in any way negative or uncomfortable with the physical side of life. True, he didn't marry, but we know that he was equally comfortable with women as with men, and counted some women among his closest friends.

There is, though, another strand, a very negative one, in ancient Judaism that I have mentioned elsewhere in this book, and that certainly had some influence on Christianity. This had to do with its difficulty in relation to some aspects of a woman's physiology, in particular menstruation. During her menstrual period a woman was considered 'unclean', and had various ritual restrictions imposed on her.

St Augustine's Teaching on Sex

It would appear that a lot of the negativity in Christian teaching about sex and the human body either had its origin, or became well established, in the writings of St Augustine in the early part of the fifth century. Augustine was one of the great teachers in the history of the church, and he wrote many wonderful things about God and his love for humanity, and how we achieve our salvation. But it has to be also acknowledged that some of his thinking was quite defective; probably most of all when it came to sex. We know that Augustine, before he was converted, had lived a fairly dissolute life, including many relationships with women that were motivated by sexual desire rather than love. After his conversion he was deeply ashamed of these, and this would seem to have coloured his teaching.

It was Augustine who definitively established the belief that sexual intercourse should take place only for the procreation of children. Sexual pleasure purely for its own sake he regarded as sinful and to be condemned. The notion that sexual pleasure might be good and that it might help a couple to deepen their love for each other was completely foreign to him. We can only speculate on how much this had to do with his personal experience. But there is no doubt that the legacy he left, denigrating any form of sexual pleasure, had a profound and long-lasting effect on church teaching. It is impossible to measure the effect it had on the marriages and individual lives of Christians for centuries, even down to our own time.

Link between Sex and Sin

But Augustine left an even more significant and unfortunate legacy. In his teaching about original sin, he made a fatal connection between sin and sexuality. Following the teaching of some other theologians of his time, he asserted that original sin was transmitted by the sexual pleasure of intercourse. This became established as the Christian understanding. From now on there was a real curse on the pleasure of sexual intercourse, and this dominated thinking in the church for a long time. Sin resulted from sex. It is no wonder that the church was so negative in its teaching about sex down through the centuries, and that so many were burdened with guilt about their sexuality. There was, of course, a double standard in this thinking. Sex was necessary in order to preserve the human race, but it was through sex that sin was inherited and perpetuated. This meant that humanity was caught in a bind. It was necessary and important to have sex, so that the human race could be continued. But in doing so sin was transmitted. People were led to believe that they were innately sinful, and that it could not be avoided. People were bad, and it was all because of sex. I suspect that this inheritance is still an influence, conscious or subconscious, on the way some church people think.

It is part of the legacy that we struggle with in trying to develop a coherent teaching on human sexuality for today's world.

We cannot blame everything on Augustine. The great Irish missionary movement that took place between the years 650 and 850 also had a part to play. These missionaries introduced the notion of the list of sins in the context of confession, which became such a feature of the Catholic church right down to our own time. There is no prize for guessing what sin featured most prominently in these lists compiled by the Irish missionaries – sex and everything to do with it. Sex became the most common matter for confession, and in its repeated telling, it began to seem even more seriously sinful. So the negative attitude to sex had already become well established in the Christian church before the end of the first millennium.

Compulsory Celibacy for Priests

The next big development was the gradual introduction of the rule of compulsory celibacy for priests. The old Jewish notion of uncleanness had never quite gone away. Gradually the rule became established that married priests should not have sexual relations with their wives for certain periods before celebrating the Eucharist. Since sexual pleasure was an evil thing, it could not be a good preparation for the Eucharist. This idea spread, until eventually the rule of compulsory celibacy for all priests was introduced, and it was promulgated for the whole church in the twelfth century. One of the great theologians of our time, Edward Schillebeeckx, in his book *The Church with a Human Face*, has this to say about the introduction of compulsory celibacy:

> Even the relatively recent law of celibacy is governed by the antiquated and ancient conviction that there is something unclean and slightly sinful about sexual intercourse (even in the context of sacramental marriage).

There was another, very practical, reason for the introduction of compulsory celibacy, which was never fully admitted by the church. We are living in the age of the politics of spin. The church had developed that to a fine art long before the politicians discovered its usefulness. By spin I mean giving a high-sounding spiritual reason for doing something that had a more material and earthly motive. By the twelfth century the church was running into difficulty with the alienation of its property. Where the married priest had a wife and children living with him in the parish house a problem often arose in the event of his death. The family could not be moved from the house. The church could not be seen to evict a widow and her children. So they were losing possession of parish houses, which necessitated providing a new dwelling for the replacement. This was becoming a big financial burden. There was an inevitable attraction in the notion of a celibate priest who, on his death, would leave no complications behind.

By this time clericalism had become established in the church, meaning that all the positions of significance and power within the church were occupied by priests or bishops. From now on decision-making within the church was in the hands of male celibates. The voices of lay people were no longer heard, particularly the voices of women. How much this affected the church's teaching and attitudes to sex is impossible to measure. But I have no doubt that it was a big influence. The New Testament is clear that celibacy is a gift from God that is only given to some. For instance, in Matthew's Gospel Jesus is quoted as saying in this context: 'Not everyone can accept this teaching, but only those to whom it is given.'

To impose celibacy as a rule for all priests brought it to an entirely different level. From being a God-given gift it was now a part of the package of priesthood. It was inevitable that some priests would not be suited to the life of celibacy and would find it an enormous burden. (They were told to pray for the gift, and it would be given to them. This contains a false logic. The church was now the arbiter of who received this gift from God. It chose to ordain men to the priesthood, and then decreed that God would give them his free gift of celibacy if they prayed hard enough.) In order to make this rule workable the church gradually developed a teaching that elevated the celibate life to a higher status than any other. The prerequisites for the promotion of celibacy were no different to the prerequisites necessary for the promotion of any type of social behaviour. Firstly, it needed the underpinning of a belief system. And so the church taught that celibacy was a higher state than marriage. From that developed the second prerequisite, the conferring of a status. If we want people to embrace new behaviour we have to give that behaviour a higher status. Status can only be attached to a position by the agreement of society. A position only has status as long as society ascribes it to the position. In ascribing status, society demands a distance between the ordinary (non-status) positions and those that contain status, and that distance is managed by ritualistic behaviour – tipping one's hat, kissing of rings, wearing special clothes. So now men would chose celibacy because it raised them above others in the community. The disadvantage of high status is that it cuts the person off both from the pleasures and the interests of the common person. Celibate priests became a special caste, different from and slightly above the ordinary person. Maintaining one's status is a delicate balancing act and demands that one denigrates the behaviour that is not allowed. So, as the new belief system took hold, and the male celibates struggled to suppress their doubts and desires, priests and bishops strongly asserted the belief that sex was not a good thing, that it was a necessary evil, to be engaged in only for the procreation of children. In all of this the legacy of Augustine was very useful, and it became the accepted doctrine. Another aspect of clericalism became evident at this point, in the sense of a type of circular thinking. Priests believed they were superior, and if that was the case, then the ordinary people were inferior and had less knowledge. Priests lost the ability to listen to anyone from outside their particular caste system, clericalism, who would challenge their views. This lasted for a long time, because it was the sort of situation that thrived in a traditional society. But in a society where most people are as well educated as the priest, status isn't as easy to maintain. And the challenge is stronger and harder to ignore. This is where the recent revelations about child abuse among some clergy have been most devastating. They undermined the commonly accepted special status of the priest.

The other thing that was inevitably at work was the personal struggle that the ordinary priest went through to suppress his desires and longings. This too promoted negative attitudes towards sex and marriage. So with the introduction of compulsory celibacy church teaching on all matters to do with sex became even more negative and restrictive. Maybe it was inevitable that celibate churchmen would try to restrict other people's enjoyment of what they could not have themselves. So the teaching that sex was only permissible for procreation became firmly established.

The 'Churching' of Mothers

The general church rejection of sex led to some other interesting developments, picking up on the Jewish idea of uncleanness, which have survived almost down to our time. Sex, even where it was permissible between married couples, or involuntary, as in the case of what we used to call 'wet dreams', excluded the person from any contact with the holy. It was around this time that communion in the hand was abolished; women were not allowed into the sanctuary, indeed during their days of menstruation they were not allowed into the church at all, nor could they receive communion. The obligation of women being 'churched' after giving birth was introduced. The idea was to cleanse them again after all the physicality of intercourse, pregnancy and birth.

By any standards all of this amounted to an extraordinary volume of negativity around the area of sex, childbirth and the human body. Of course the big question is to what extent church teaching today is still influenced by these types of attitudes.

Humanae Vitae *and the Contraception Issue*

Some readers might be thinking that this is all in the past and has no relevance to our lives, but recent events would suggest that church teaching hasn't really changed that much, even though society and the lives of people have changed dramatically. Before the Second Vatican Council was convened there were a number of burning issues, relating to sex and marriage, which were being hotly discussed. Probably the main ones were the use of artificial contraception within marriage, and the pastoral care of people who were divorced and remarried. Many of the bishops attending the council had hoped that these issues would be discussed openly, and decisions made on them, during the council. But that did not happen. Through the influence of the Curia, and the submission of the pope to Curial pressure, none of the controversial issues were dealt with. This is typical of what governments do when any issue is controversial or where political fallout is feared. It shows again the church following the model of earthly power. As we know the contraception question was taken off the council agenda, and put in the hands of a commission. This commission duly reported a few years later. There was a large majority in favour of change. But a small minority of members were so determined in their views that they refused to accept the opinions of the majority and instead sent in their own minority report. The pope at the time, Pope Paul VI, agonised over it for a long time, and eventually made a judgement in line with the minority report, retaining the ban on artificial contraceptives. It met with widespread disapproval both in the theological community and among the faithful generally. To quote just one theologian, in order to give a flavour of the strength of reaction at the time, Johannes Neumann, a German, called it a statement 'consisting of an inappropriate medley of Platonic, Aristotelian and Thomistic ideas, which is going beyond its brief and can claim neither obedience nor credibility'.

The background to *Humanae Vitae* is explained very clearly by Bernard Haring, one of the members of the commission set up by Paul VI:

> After years of dispute, in 1929 the Lambeth conference (of the Anglican church) officially decided that contraception was a morally acceptable compromise solution, provided some essential criteria were met. A year later there were harsh reprisals from Rome. Pius XI felt he had to confront the Anglican community and similar efforts in other reformed churches; so he insisted on the strict Augustinian line. His encyclical 'Casti Conubii' explicitly labelled contraception a crime. By a wide majority, the commission that Pope Paul VI set up to deal with population issues voted to revise 'Casti Conubii'. But the spokesman for the minority felt it was unthinkable that the Holy Spirit might be working more effectively with the Anglicans at the Lambeth conference than with the pope of Rome. This peculiar attitude shows how difficult a transition it was and is (especially for church officials) from a theology of controversy to inter-confessional dialogue and willingness to learn from others.

One of the very interesting side effects of the whole *Humanae Vitae* controversy is that it led to a major debate on the use of authority in the church, which may in the long run be the most beneficial aspect of the whole event. Even though, a few short years before, the Vatican Council had called on the pope to act collegially, meaning in consultation with the bishops, in this instance he acted on his own, or at most with the advice of a small group of people holding a minority view. The notion of collegiality was undoubtedly a casualty of this decision.

This issue highlights two problems that have bedevilled church teaching for many centuries. Firstly, as Haring illustrates, too much church teaching has been drawn up in an adversarial spirit, with the focus on contradicting one or other of the Reformation churches rather than genuinely searching for the truth. It is questionable whether Catholic teaching on artificial contraception might not be different if other Christian churches had not first taken up a position on it.

Secondly, the belief that the church can never err meant that they found themselves in a dilemma entirely of their own making – one pope could not be seen to contradict another. This, at the very least, greatly influenced the final decision. It is hard not to feel sorry for the Holy Spirit, trying to give the true message with so many other agendas at work.

Changing Attitudes Regarding Sex and Relationships

There has been a big change in thinking on sex and relationships in the church in the last thirty years or so. But this change of thinking has not been universally accepted within the church. At the official level little has changed, but at the level of theology, and in the lives of the ordinary believers, there is radical new thinking going on. One of the big problems of the past thirty years has been this divergence between official teaching, theological reflection, and the views of the ordinary Catholic. The new theological thinking has amounted in some ways to a volte face. Instead of seeing sex as something negative, intrinsically associated with sin, Catholic church theology today talks about the beauty and goodness of the sexual relationship in marriage. It allows the husband and wife to actually enjoy themselves during sex, and asserts that this pleasure is not only not sinful, but that it is good. It freely accepts that an intimate sexual relationship can help husband and wife to grow in their love for each other. It teaches that the primary purpose of sex in marriage is the promotion of love between the couple, with procreation relegated to a secondary, though still important, role. It is no longer claimed, as it was consistently in the past, that a celibate life is superior to marriage, that celibacy is a more holy state that will earn a greater reward in Heaven. Now, if anything, the balance has gone the other way, for the simple reason that so much work has been put into the development of the theology of marriage, whereas little enough attention has been given to the theology of celibacy. Instead celibacy has become a source of controversy, with the 'liberals' calling for the abolition of compulsory celibacy, and the 'traditionalists' arguing for its retention.

Huge tension has resulted, and the tensions have been unresolved partly again because the church will not admit to error – the self-same reason that has caused much of the stagnation within the church. The official church argues for the retention of celibacy on the grounds that Jesus was a celibate, and that celibacy leaves a person free to devote themselves to God and to the people in a way that a married person cannot. Weak and unconvincing arguments such as these result in a loss of credibility. All of this controversy, and confrontational attitudes, has made it impossible to develop a better theology of celibacy.

Of course it was inevitable that when the church accepted the first and basic purpose of sex in marriage as the promotion of the relationship, the issue of contraception would become a burning one. If a couple can only have sex when they want to have a child, then sex will be a very rare occurrence in a marriage, and this would severely restrict something that is essential for the good of the marriage. So the church can be accused of contradicting itself here. In order to try to get around this, the church did its best to promote natural means of contraception. For a woman who had a fear of pregnancy, for whatever reason, the natural methods did not give anything like the sort of assurance needed for her to relax and enjoy sex. Sex for that woman was an anxious, fearful act rather than a loving one, and as such it was counterproductive. It served to cause discord rather than promote love in the marriage. The English moral theologian, Kevin T. Kelly, in a recent article in *The Furrow*, quotes from a survey done in France around the time of *Humanae Vitae*, asking Catholic couples about their experience of natural methods of birth control:

> One thing stands out in my mind from reading their replies. 'Cauchemar', a French word which I did not know, was used repeatedly and always in the same context – a woman describing how she experienced sexual intercourse when she was fearful of becoming pregnant again. I soon discovered that it meant 'nightmare'. That spoke volumes to me. If anything was grossly immoral, it was ethical teaching which resulted in many women experiencing the act of love-making as a nightmare.

Natural methods have their place in planning a family, but to burden them with being the only permissible form of birth control was clearly asking far too much. At their best they had a limited use.

I think at this point it would be hard to argue with Bernard Haring's estimate that the decision of Pope Paul VI to go with the minority report and write *Humanae Vitae* was 'a tragic decision'. Recalling Haring's reflections on the doctrine of infallibility, clearly this teaching was not 'received' by the vast majority of Catholics. And if we assume that the Spirit speaks not just through the pope, but thought all the faithful, then that must be a fairly convincing proof of the mistake that the pope made. It is important to acknowledge here that many practising Catholics, people close to the church, struggled to put this teaching into practice, but found themselves unable to do so. It was the real beginning of the ordinary faithful losing faith in the church's ability to speak or teach on sex and relationships. By now they have moved to what is possibly the other extreme, a position that is also problematic. The faithful have created a new belief system; they have come to believe that the official church is no longer credible in this area, and that they know better. It also started something that has since become very common, the notion of the ordinary faithful questioning the value of a life of celibacy, and the degree to which it makes a person incapable of understanding real life. By clinging to old ways of thinking even in the face of enormous change, the church started to lose credibility. And from once that slide began, and people got into the habit of questioning church decisions, the mystique of church authority was punctured, and things would definitely never be the same again.

The recent revelation of what have become known as 'the scandals', the fact that some priests and religious had sexually and physically abused children in parishes and in institutions, has greatly accelerated this trend. The fact that the revelations about such abuse happened at a time when people had learned, after hundreds of years of silent submission, to question the church, complicated the matter. After years of authoritarianism a great amount of resentment had built up against the church, and the scandals have given people a free rein to express their pent up anger and resentment.

The Virgin Birth

The question of virginity and its place in church teaching is another issue that I believe the Catholic church needs to revisit. For centuries the church has praised the state of virginity as a high and holy state, when it is adopted for the sake of the Kingdom of God. This of course fitted in well with the enforcement of celibacy for priests. As part of the elevation of virginity, it proclaimed Mary, the mother of God, as the perfect example of virginity, since our faith declares that she gave birth to her son without having intercourse with any human person; and that, having given birth to Jesus, she remained a virgin for the rest of her life, and did not have sexual relations even with her husband, or give birth to any further children. This has become accepted as the Catholic understanding of Mary, and for centuries devotion to her as the 'virgin most pure' has been popular.

But my understanding is that many reputable Scripture scholars today accept that the story of the birth of Jesus, as recounted in the Gospels of Matthew and Luke, is probably not an historical account of how Jesus came to be born. It is not valid to read these stories as accurate descriptions of actual events. The great colossus of Catholic Bible study, Raymond Brown, wrote about all this in his seminal work, *The Birth of the Messiah*, almost thirty years ago. It is a difficult book, and in the best academic tradition he does not come down strongly on either side. He will only go so far as to say that:

> The scientifically controllable biblical evidence leaves the question of the historicity of the virginal conception unresolved.

A more readable and popular version of the subject, *The First Christmas*, by H. J. Richards was published about the same time. He puts the position more simply and clearly. I will try briefly to summarise what he says: The Nativity story was a later addition to the Gospels, written well after the time of Jesus, and later than the rest of the Gospels. It is a theological, not a historical statement. It is saying very important things about Jesus, not about Mary. The main point the author wished to emphasise was the divine origin of Jesus. To do that he drew on ancient myths, popular at the time, about how great heroes were born without human intervention, in other words coming directly from God. He also drew on many Old Testament themes, and very many of the sentences and images in the story are taken directly from the Old Testament. He wanted to show that Jesus fitted in with the Old

Testament prophecies about the coming of a Messiah. Jesus is the Christ, the promised one, sent by God to be the Saviour. The author would have known very well that his readers at the time would not have taken this as historical reality, but as a statement of immense significance about Jesus.

Why did they depict Mary as a virgin in the story? Partly it was following other mythological stories prevalent at the time. This person was of such significance that he came directly from God. But there was another reason. In Old Testament times virginity was not a prized and honoured state as Christianity later came to regard it. Rather it was considered a barren, non-productive, and shameful condition. Richards puts it well:

> Perhaps the point could best be made by quoting a few lines from the Litany of Loreto, which we Catholics have long been used to say or sing in honour of our Lady:
>
> Virgin most prudent
> Virgin most venerable
> Virgin most renowned
> Virgin most powerful
> Virgin most faithful
>
> Speaking biblically these are entirely the wrong categories, as if virginity was something to be proud of and kept intact. On the contrary, in biblical terms we would have to say:
>
> Virgin most foolish!
> Virgin most humiliated!
> Virgin most despised!
> Virgin most weak!
> Virgin most fruitless!

The point Richards is making is that the writer chose the image of barren virginity to show how wonderful was the work of God, that he could bring such glorious fruit out of emptiness. In the Gospel story there is a close connection made between the image of the empty womb (the virgin) and the empty tomb (at Easter). Out of emptiness comes the Saviour.

Read in this way, the nativity story takes on a new and wonderful meaning. It is not about virginity. Rather it is a glorious statement about Jesus, his divine origin and purpose. But the other side of the coin is that it raises the possibility that Jesus was born in the same way as any other human being, as a result of the loving relationship between Mary and Joseph. Modern scholars, like Jerome Murphy-O'Connor seem to suggest, though, as far as I know, without stating it directly, that Mary might have had more children. That would be a fairly natural assumption if we accept that the story of the Virgin Birth is not historically accurate. If Jesus was born in the normal human way to Mary and Joseph, they would in all probability have had more children if it was possible for them. They were living in a society that valued large families, and regarded barrenness as a sign of God's disfavour. The Gospels do state quite specifically that Jesus had brothers and sisters, who, incidentally, didn't take too kindly at times to his ministry. One of his brothers, James, took over the leadership of the early Christian community in Jerusalem after Peter.

Was Mary Really a Virgin?
What we have here is something quite complicated and difficult. At the theological and scholarly level something is being studied and suggested, though it is fair to say that Scripture scholars are very cautious in writing about it. They treat the topic gingerly, knowing it is very controversial. They write about it in academic journals and books, in a way that suggests to me that they wish to keep the topic among themselves, and do nothing that might disturb the simple faith of the people in the Virgin Mary. They back away from trying to bridge that gap, and educate the people in

the scriptural understanding. This is because devotion to Mary is even more emotionally charged in the Catholic church than devotion to Christ. There is also the further complication that the virginity of Mary is one of the defined doctrines of our faith.

Both Richards and Brown try to deal with that by stating that the origin of the church doctrine on the virginity of Mary was not a biological statement. Brown puts it this way:

> The virginal conception under its creedal title of 'virgin birth' is not primarily a biological statement, and therefore one must make a judgement about the extent to which the creedal affirmation is inextricably attached to the biological presupposition.

He goes on to make two further points that are worth quoting:

> First, in orthodox Christian belief, Jesus would be God's Son no matter how he was conceived, since his is an eternal sonship not dependent upon the incarnation. Second, for ordinary Christians the virginal conception has proved an effective interpretative sign of that eternal divine sonship; and we should not underestimate the adverse pedagogical impact on the understanding of divine sonship if the virginal conception is denied.

This language is difficult and oblique. I am quoting Raymond Brown because he is the acknowledged expert on these matters. I can't help thinking that he writes in this way so that those of us who are not Scripture scholars will not understand it and in this way his opinions will be kept safely within the confines of the academic community. I think that what Raymond Brown is saying is that people's faith would be undermined by the suggestion that Mary might not have been a virgin. This stance may have been permissible in the past, but with today's highly educated believers it is no longer adequate. Ultimately whether or not Mary was a virgin would make no difference at all to the divinity of

Jesus. The way God chose to send his Son into the world is irrelevant. What is important is that he came. If our faith in the divinity of Jesus depended on believing that Mary was a virgin, and that God was the direct, physical father of Jesus, we would be on very shaky ground. It would make some sense if we still believed that the male sperm contained the full human in embryo, and that the female only provided the receptacle for growth, as people believed at the time when this doctrine originated. Now we know that it is the fusion of the male and female that creates the embryo. If we were working off that logic, all we could say is that Jesus would be part divine and part human. But our faith does not depend on any of this. Jesus, the Son of God, came into the world through the loving action of the Father. The details of how God brought this about are not significant.

I know that suggesting Mary might not be virgin in the physical sense would be interpreted by many people as degrading her. This is a clear indication that the old belief system about the superiority of celibacy and virginity is still very much in place. But I think it is a very unhealthy situation for everyone, and especially for the faith, if there is a different understanding between the scholars and the faithful. My main point is that it is not the fact of this teaching that is the problem. It is the use that has been made of it down through the centuries. The notion of Mary's virginity, and the elevation of the state of virginity, has been massively influential in shaping church teaching and attitudes towards sex. Imagine the difference it would have made if the ordinary Catholic had believed that Mary was a married woman, having normal sexual relationships with her husband, and rearing her children. We would have to change our whole image of the home of Nazareth, and populate it with maybe four or five children rather than one. It would have totally altered our view of the married woman. She would have been seen as equal, if not superior, to the virgin. Catholic teaching on sex, marriage and ministry would have been radically different.

Jungian psychology suggests that the prominence given to the idea of virginity in traditional Catholic teaching has caused problems for both women and men. The suggestion is that Catholicism has had difficulty in seeing female sexuality as something good and positive. Mary was thought to have had a child without having sex, and has been exalted because of it. Into the woman's consciousness has seeped the idea that perfect motherhood does not entail sexual intercourse. Her goodness is diminished by having sex, even with her husband. The traditional Catholic male, maybe subconsciously, believes that the ideal woman does not have sexual intercourse. The male is then left with the problem as to how he can express his sexual drive. For him it becomes increasingly difficult to integrate sexuality and goodness in his image of the woman. So he tends to see the woman either as the 'Mary' image of perfect goodness and purity, or else as a sex object. (The famous quote of Pope St Gregory the Great is useful here: 'woman's use is two-fold: animal sex and motherhood'.)

I don't know to what extent Jung's view is true (and the supposedly liberated attitude to sex in post-Christian societies is not the perfect answer either), but I do believe that the more real and rounded image of Mary that I suggest above would be healthier for all of us.

Where do we go from Here?
There are no simple solutions to the problems I have raised in this chapter. It is clear that our teaching and attitudes to sex and human relationships in the church carry an enormous amount of baggage from the past. Beliefs that were both wrong and destructive were prevalent for much of the history of the church. They have undoubtedly influenced church teaching and thinking down to the present. We have taken many of them from sources other than the teaching of Christ. Great damage has been done to peo-

ple, and particularly to women. Great damage has also been done to the Christian message, and we have lost credibility; many people do not listen to us when we speak on human sexuality any more. And yet it is an area where humanity desperately needs help and guidance.

We could begin by acknowledging our mistakes, and that needs to be done at the highest level in the church. Then it is essential that we overcome our fear, and allow for an open expression of views and opinions. This will neither be easy nor pleasant. Sexuality generates so much emotion, and is difficult to discuss rationally. But I do not see any other way of helping us to get out of our current impasse. Ultimately it has to do with trusting the Holy Spirit. A period of open, free exchange of ideas, with strong and decisive leadership coming from the top and resisting the inevitable efforts to stifle opinion, is the only way forward. It will not be easy for many people. Devotion to Mary is so closely tied up with the idea of virginity that it would be hard for people to let go. But I am confident that in the long run it would lead to a more real and fruitful devotion. It would be easier to relate to Mary, the married woman and mother of a family.

Unfortunately I don't believe that any of this can happen in the present climate in the church. There is far too much repression and fear. Some of the other, more fundamental, changes that I suggest in other parts of this book will have to come about first. Only then will we be able to begin to clarify church teaching on sexuality and relationships, and make them more credible.

VI

CONFESSION AS A MEANS OF CONTROL

Recently, I was saying mass in an old-style psychiatric institution that was gradually being phased out. About sixty of the remaining residents gathered for mass, and I, a missioner in the parish, was the celebrant. My fellow missioner said that he would come and hear a few confessions, if any wished to go, but he would be a little late arriving. I had begun the mass when he entered the back door of the small church. So I introduced him and as he walked up the church I told the people present that he would go into the confession box and be available for anyone who wished to receive the sacrament. By the time I had finished my introduction he had arrived at the box, and opened the door. A vacuum cleaner fell out on top of him. The first penitent, who had moved quickly to get to the top of the queue, opened the other side of the box and brushes and brooms fell out on top of him. The confession box was being used for storage. It is an image of the state of the sacrament in today's church.

'Bless me, Father, for I have sinned ...' That sentence has a deep resonance for generations of Catholics. It provokes a host of memories, carries with it a particular smell of the enclosed timber box, and maybe most of all the darkness. The sensation when the slide is pulled over is something we will take with us to our grave. There is inevitably at least some degree of anxiety associated with those memories. What sort of person would be behind that slide? Would he be kind, or harsh? Would he understand my situation, and be helpful in his advice, or would he condemn?

For most of us now these are only memories. We rarely, if ever, go into confession boxes any more. They stand idle in most churches, or are used, as in the above situation, as storage space. There are still a few places, like shrines or religious churches, where confessions in this traditional format are still being heard, but I think it is fair to say that these are remnants of the past rather than a sign of the future.

A Flash Point of Debate

It is significant that the sacrament of penance, or as it was commonly called, confession is one of the flash points of the debate and struggle going on in the Catholic church at the moment. This is as it should be, because confession was in the front line of what was both good and bad about the traditional church. Not long ago one of the Irish bishops, in his Lenten Pastoral, called for his people to return to the traditional practice of confession. He said that confession was not properly celebrated unless people told their sins in detail, and not just according to a general formula. At the same time a Dublin parish priest, in an article in *The Furrow*, was saying the exact opposite. He was recommending that people be encouraged to go to confession using a general statement of their sinfulness rather than feeling that they had to go into a detailed telling of their sins. He advocated this in particular for people who experienced any type of anxiety or stress in relation to confession, and that, I suspect, includes most Catholics over a certain age.

The practice of confession now varies widely in this country. In two parishes where I recently worked on consecutive weeks the contrast was striking. In our missions we usually do a community celebration of the sacrament with an opportunity for individual confession, but briefly and using general statements rather than giving a list of sins. Priests stand around and the people approach, make a general statement of their sinfulness, mention a specific item or two if they wish, and receive absolution. It is a nice ceremony when done well, and helps to bring the focus back to God and his forgiveness rather than the sins of the penitent. In the first parish the priest was uneasy with this, and would only agree to let us do it if we promised to also spend time in the confessional boxes so that people could confess in that way if they wished. In the next parish, when I explained what we usually did, the priest informed me that for the past eight years he had given general absolution to his people twice a year, and that was what he wished me to do. I have learned over the years the importance of being flexible in my work.

It does not surprise me that confession is an issue between those who want to call the church back to the old ways and those who want to move on to something new. The practice of confession as we have known it in recent centuries has been one of the most effective ways in which the very powerful church exercised its power over the people. As the great moral theologian, Bernard Haring, said:

> The sacrament of confession became a particularly vivid symbol of a judging and controlling church.

The Development of Confession

Confession was slow in developing, and has seen many different forms down through the centuries. It would be a mistake to think that the form my generation grew up with in the middle of the last century was the way it had been from the beginning. On the contrary, that form of frequent, devotional confession had a relatively short history. In the early centuries of the church confession was practised very infrequently. Its earliest form occurred when the community of believers expelled someone from their group who had committed some action which caused public scandal and brought reprobation on the community as a whole. It was the community who administered the sacrament, and channelled

God's forgiveness to the sinner. But the focus was more on the good name of the community, and as such the forgiveness was given only when the community was assured that there was a real change of life, and that the person would not bring disgrace on the community again. For this reason that early form of confession is not a good illustration of the forgiveness of God. The needs of the community meant that there were two very separate and different agendas at work. On the one hand, the community was controlling the behaviour of its members, while at the same time, taking on the power to forgive sin. I think that was a pity, because it introduced the idea of confession as a means of control, and that idea became more and more prominent as the centuries passed, until it became in our time, as Haring said, the great means of power for a controlling church. It is hard to reconcile the notion of confession as a means of controlling behaviour with the teaching of Christ who called people to repent, but always of their own free will.

Private Confession

Private confession only began some hundreds of years after Jesus, and grew out of the very close relationship between monks in monasteries and the local people living in the vicinity. People were in the habit of going to the monastery and asking the monks for help in all the different circumstances of their lives. They asked for material help, they asked for prayers in times of trouble, they looked for assurance of God's forgiveness of their sins, and asked for encouragement in their efforts to change. In those times there was only one ordained minister in the monastery, whose job was to preside at the Eucharist. The other monks would not have been priests, but that did not prevent them from being the mediator through whom people were assured that their sins were forgiven. In fact it was only in the ninth century that the hearing of confession was restricted to priests. I suspect that this practice, even though it was localised and only available to people in the vicinity of monasteries, was the closest the church has come at any stage in its history to celebrating the sacrament properly. There were no rules and laws dictating when and how it should be done. It was totally in the service of the needs of the penitent. He or she felt burdened by what they had done, and needed to express that in words and be assured of the forgiveness of God. In the Gospels the penitent came to Jesus. He did not coerce them in any way; he asked no questions; he received them with compassion and said: 'Your sins are forgiven; go in peace and do not sin again.' The simplicity of the encounter is what makes it profound.

The practice of confession as we have known it only became widely available to the ordinary believers around the eight century when confession boxes were introduced into churches. Historians tend to give the credit, if that is the appropriate word for this development, to the great Irish missionary movement of that era, the period that earned Ireland the title 'Island of Saints and Scholars'. It was the period of restoration in Europe after the time that historians call the Dark Ages which followed the collapse of the Roman Empire in the fifth and sixth centuries. During those 'dark ages', characterised by a collapse of the social and religious order that had been built up during the Roman Empire, many churches had been destroyed, but were now being rebuilt, and confession boxes were put into them. Since priests in those times were often not well educated, and were poorly prepared for this new form of ministry, manuals were written for confessors. These contained the initial form of what became very common in the church up to recent times, namely lists of sins. This probably seemed a very sensible thing to do at the time, but it hindsight it was an unfortunate development. The listing of sins was designed to meet the needs of the confessor, to help him define what was a sin and what wasn't and how serious a particular sin might be, and not the needs of the penitent. From now on the sacrament

gradually developed in such a way that it fulfilled the requirements of a legalistic church rather than a penitent burdened down
with sorrow and guilt. It became ritualised into reciting off a list
of sins or misdemeanours which were often fairly meaningless and
bore little enough relation to what was really going on in a person's life. This happened slowly over the centuries, and the style
of confession that was popular until recent times, known as devotional confession, goes back a couple of hundred years. Devotional confession means going to confession in order to receive the
grace of the sacrament rather than having any particular sin that
needed to be told. It was designed to facilitate the practice of frequent confession, which was considered to be a good thing to do
at the time. I can remember sermons from my youth in praise of
people who went to confession every day. Now I would look back
on this practice and regard it as a highly suspect and somewhat
neurotic thing to do. It was a good example of what happened in
what we could call that very sacramental era in the church. The
sacraments, which are intended to be high-points or celebrations
of an ever-present reality, namely that God is always present to us
in our human condition, came to be seen as the sole manifestation of that reality. In other words, instead of confession being a
celebration of the fact that God was constantly pouring out his
mercy on sinners, it came to be seen instead as the only, and consequently essential, channel of forgiveness.

Weakness of this Style of Confession

There were three main problems associated with the style of
'devotional confession' that was practised in the nineteenth and
twentieth centuries.

The first problem is that it gave a false impression of God's
mercy. It introduced the concept of a 'good' or a 'bad' confession.
We were told that there were a great number of conditions we
had to perform correctly in order to make a good confession. We

had to tell all our sins; we had to tell them in sufficient detail so
that the confessor could make an accurate judgement of the nature of the sins, whether they were mortal or venial; we had to
tell the amount of times we had committed those sins since our
last confession. We were in dread of making a bad confession. A
lot of this had to do with the fact that the confessor saw himself
as the judge of the penitent, an idea that was introduced after the
Reformation. The idea was that the confessor needed to know
everything about the sin, so that he could judge whether or not
to grant forgiveness, and what type of penance to give. It was a
very unfortunate development. Instead of being the instrument,
the channel, of God's mercy, the confessor was now putting himself in the place of God, deciding if forgiveness would be granted.
The underlying message of all of this was clear. God's mercy was
presented as being miserly, hard to obtain, and surrounded by conditions. Instead of the limitless, unconditional mercy that is the
Biblical picture, we had made God in our own image. He was
someone who was slow to forgive, even slower to forget.

Scrupulosity
The second problem with this style of confession is that it promoted scrupulosity. To quote Bernard Haring:

> This practice fostered an explosion of scrupulosity that was unique
> in the history of Christianity. In order to be certain of forgiveness
> and salvation, one had to confess all serious sins, their number and
> nature, along with any circumstances that might alter the case.
> Handbooks of moral theology had such a long and complicated cata-
> logue of transgressions that anxious penitents, especially in the
> hands of an unskilled confessor, could never decide whether they
> had really confessed all their sins.

Things became really difficult when a scrupulous penitent happened to meet a scrupulous confessor. There was no limit to the

depth of confusion this could cause. A story goes that one such confessor was particularly concerned about getting an accurate account of the number of times a sin had been committed. Having questioned the penitent carefully he tended to solve the problem by suggesting: 'Will we settle for a million?' He solved the immediate problem, but hardly gave a good image of the forgiving God.

Fear

The third difficulty with this style of confession is that it generated fear. Fear was very much a part of religion at the time, and it was instilled in many ways. Preaching often set out to make people fearful, by vivid descriptions of the fires of Hell, and the punishments that would be meted out to the damned by the devils. Often the impression was given that Hell would be the final outcome for most people, and that only a few got into Heaven. A sense of despair and hopelessness could be generated. Confession, because of its nature as a one-to-one encounter, was probably the most effective weapon for generating fear. Again Bernard Haring has strong words to say about this type of religious practice:

> In almost all religions, including Catholicism, there was and still is a temptation to use the potent motive of fear, forcing people to toe the line in religion and other things. It is a satanic notion to exploit the name of God and Christ to make people submissive through feelings of anxiety, even if this exploitation is for a noble cause.

Undoubtedly what he has to say here applies to the practice of confession in recent centuries in the church. Anxiety and fear were used in the way the sacrament was celebrated to make people submissive, and to keep them under control. The right of people to think for themselves, and make the final judgements on their own lives was not recognised.

Haring continues:

Add to that fear the massive threat of eternal punishment in Hell for every more or less voluntary trespass, and a tremendous, paralysing potential for anxiety might develop. But, beyond that, all the available attention of Christians was fascinated and monopolised by this multitude of menacing laws and bans. In the end there was scarcely any creative energy left for constructive, liberating and healing action.

That sentence resonates strongly with me. In the course of my early life as a priest I spent many hours in confession boxes with people who were full of anxiety about their salvation because of some tendency or weakness they were struggling with. For instance the problem of masturbation. To teach that every act of masturbation is a mortal sin, punishable by the eternal fires of Hell, was an extraordinary and oppressive thing to do. It created untold anxiety, tension and depression in men, in particular. And the ironic thing was that the more anxious and depressed they became over their state of serious sin, the less they were able to resist the action. The tension inside them became so great that it had to find some form of release. For these people the Christian message was not a word of liberation, but of slavery.

Haring makes a crucially important corrective in all of this. Putting too much emphasis on sin is not a proper reflection on the teaching of Jesus. Our emphasis, according to Haring, should be on salvation, and not just on the salvation of the individual person, which he classifies as a selfish motive for good living ('those who think only of their own freedom are and remain slaves of egoism') but the salvation of all humanity. I was delighted to read this statement from Haring. I have always been uncomfortable with the notion of individual salvation. The leaflet produced for Redemptorist missions in the generation before my time had the sentence: 'You have one life to live, one soul to save …'

I have never been able to accept that a person could be happy in Heaven if a large section of humanity, including some of their own acquaintances, were condemned to Hell for all eternity.

Jesus and Sinners

Looking at the encounters Jesus had with sinners gives us some idea of how the sacrament of penance or reconciliation should be celebrated. First we need to realise that the word 'sinner' was a much stronger word in the society in which Jesus lived than it is for us today. When a person was branded a sinner in those days it tended to be a final judgement. There was no way back, no forgiveness, either by religion or society. When Jesus met the woman caught in adultery, the woman at the home of Simon the Pharisee, probably the woman at the well in Samaria, and the tax-collector Zaccheus, he was meeting people who were outcasts, despised by the people. But he was someone who was completely free from the prejudices and judgements of his time. He had a different way of looking at life and people. It is very obvious and significant that he never asked anyone what they had done. He showed no interest whatever in the nature or the amount of their sin. So how did the church get to the stage where it made the detailed reciting of sins a necessary condition of forgiveness? It seems such a strange thing to insist on, considering the example of Jesus. It is interesting to reflect on how Jesus might treat the modern pariahs of our society, the drug barons, and the child abusers. He would forgive them but say to them as he said to the woman taken in adultery, 'Go, and sin no more'. I know that in writing this I run the risk of being accused of saying that there is nothing wrong with drug pushing or child abuse. I'm not saying that: I'm contrasting society's view with that of Christ, who said: 'My ways are not your ways'.

The other thing that was notable about Jesus is that he didn't doubt or question people about their good will, their awareness of their sinfulness and their desire for forgiveness. He seemed to take their presence as sufficient sign that they were well disposed. They didn't have to prove anything to him. And he was certainly not there to judge. Again we must wonder how the church, in light of the clear example of Jesus, developed a theology of the priest as judge, deciding to either give or withhold forgiveness. Jesus set out to give sinners a new image of themselves; he helped them to see themselves and life differently. They all left his presence feeling better, standing taller, and clearly believing in their own worth and value. He also encouraged them to live in a new way. 'Go in peace, and do not sin again'. A life of sin is a destructive life, and Jesus wanted them to recognise that, and to see that there is a better way. So the encounter of the sinner with Jesus was marked by a great sense of relief and joy on the part of the sinner, a new perspective on themselves and their lives, and a feeling of hope about the future, a feeling that change just might be possible. Those are the features we need to replicate in the way we celebrate the sacrament. Sadly, for many people at different times in the history of the church, this has not been the case.

From my work as a priest I am very aware of how the practice of the church in the sacrament of confession has contrasted sharply and sadly with the example of Jesus. A typical illustration from today's world is the situation of the couple who are involved in a second relationship, after one or other marriage has broken up, and who are also committed members of the church. When a person in that situation goes to confession they can unfortunately meet a confessor who will give them a less than compassionate reception. The priest who sees himself as judge will tend to pronounce a negative judgement on them, and rule that they are not eligible for forgiveness unless they renounce their current relationship. In doing this the priest is taking over the role of the penitent's conscience, and making his life decisions for him. Nobody has the right to do this. Instead of being the minister of God's mercy, he has assumed instead the role of God. Once again it is hard to see how the example of Jesus justifies this type of attitude. But maybe it is wrong to lay too much blame at the door of the priest. The message coming from every official church document on this subject is that people in second relationships must not receive the sacraments, must not be admitted to the full life of the church, but can only receive the forgiveness of God if they cease to have a sexual relationship with their current partner. It is a further example of how the church continues to be obsessed with matters of a sexual nature. We are less likely to hear the church forbidding the sacraments to people who are involved in other forms of 'immoral' lifestyle.

A Better Celebration on God's Forgiveness

So what must we do to better celebrate and channel the forgiveness of God? A lot of change has taken place in the past twenty years, and a number of new ways have been attempted. This has been good. Communal celebrations of the sacrament, with the opportunity of a brief encounter with the priest, have now become the norm in many places. They have greatly helped to free people, and take the fear and anxiety out of confession. In doing this they have achieved something that was very necessary. But I do not see this method of celebrating the sacrament as a satisfactory way of the future. Rather I see it as a transitional solution, necessary because of the negative experiences of so many in the past. I have two suggestions for a way forward.

There is undoubtedly a human need for individual confession. But that human need is not something that arises every week or month. The practice of going to confession every week or month was an imposition of the church rather than something that arose from human need. There are occasional times in life when a person may be burdened by some guilt or failure that needs to be talked out. That person may need the reassurance of God's mercy to be given in a human one-to-one encounter. Maybe some ad-

vice might be sought. There should be a facility for this. But the
penitent should not have to say how long since their last confession. That is irrelevant. The length of time since the person has
been to confession is of no importance whatsoever. The penitent
is the only one who can decide when and if they need this form
of the sacrament, and what they want to confess. We must also
get rid of the notion of the priest as judge. Let the confessor be
purely and simply the agent of God's forgiveness. If he is asked for
advice, he can give it to the best of his ability, but no more than
that. He is there to lay his hands on the penitent and speak the
reassuring words of Jesus. 'Your sins are forgiven; go in peace and
do not sin again'. The church, through its confessor, must be seen
as totally trusting the penitent, receiving her or him with compassion, and leaving all matters of judgement to God.

In conjunction with this style of confession, which of its nature will be very occasional in a person's life, there is need for
another form, which would be available on a more regular basis
as a celebration of the mercy of God. For this I am suggesting that
we could return to a practice of the medieval church. Twice a
year bishops and abbots gave general absolution to all the faithful. (Some historians suggest that abbesses gave it also.) That could
be re-introduced, with maybe the authority given to the parish
priest. And let us resist the temptation to hedge it around with
too many, or indeed any, conditions. Apparently in the ancient
practice the only condition was that a person who had committed a sin that was also a civil crime would need to go to individual confession. That was a clear and easily understood condition.

I think a combination of both those styles of confession would
serve the church well into the future. We would see an end to unhealthy control, an end to judgement by the priest, an end to fear
and anxiety. Instead the sacrament would become what it is intended to be, a celebration of the unfathomable mercy of God.
More than any other sacrament confession is the one that con-

tains the loveliest message. Properly celebrated, it is the greatest manifestation of God's love for misfortunate humanity, the covenant that prefigures Heaven, where every tear is wiped away, the veil is pulled back and we see God face to face. The fact that he forgives our sins must be the most wonderful revelation imaginable. It is undoubtedly something to celebrate.

VII

MINISTRY IN THE CHURCH

I am a native of a small, largely rural, diocese in the west of Ireland. It is made up of about twenty-five parishes, most of which had two priests when I was young but are now served by one older man. It is a good few years since there was a student for the priesthood from this diocese, and there is nobody currently in training. All the indications are that in twenty years' time most of these parishes will no longer have a resident priest to say mass for them. Each of the parishes has their own definite identity and a strong community spirit. To be left without a priest would be a big blow to them. What is the solution to this problem? Assuming that the downward trend in vocations to the priesthood will not change dramatically in that space of time, what can be done? There seem to me to be two possible answers. One would be to bring in priests from some countries, like Nigeria for instance, where they are plentiful. The other answer would be to redefine the notion of ministry, to change the requirements for priesthood, maybe to open it up to married people, and women.

In this chapter I want to look at the question of priesthood, or ministry in the church. In order to do this I will need to retrace my steps a little, and state again some of the basic historical facts about the early church, because they are immensely relevant to this question.

Did Jesus Ordain Priests?

I think it is valid to assert that Jesus did not establish a ministerial priesthood. As I outlined in an earlier chapter, it is not even very certain that he intended setting up a church, and if he did, what kind of church he had in mind. The only thing that can be said for certain is that he gave his followers a project, a mission. They were to go out and preach the Kingdom of God, while at the same time healing people of all their ailments. So he definitely had this missionary aspect to his ministry, this urge to go and spread the message, and he wanted it to continue after his departure. The coming of the Holy Spirit and the gift of speech and new courage given to the close followers who were gathered in that upper room after the resurrection clearly seems to indicate that.

I've shown elsewhere that ministry in the early communities of believers was a diverse thing, with many people, men and women, involved and taking responsibility for different functions and services. The leader of the Eucharistic celebration would not necessarily be the one with the gift of preaching or teaching. And somebody else entirely could be involved in the ministry of caring for the poorer members of the community, the 'widows and orphans' as the New Testament classified them. Another person again would look after the practical and financial affairs of the community. Judging by the Gospels, Jesus didn't have great admiration for the priests in the Jewish religion, the men who looked after the temple. They became his greatest enemies, their enmity undoubtedly fuelled by the incident where he cleared the traders from the temple precincts using a whip. It was they, led by the chief priest, Caiaphas, who were instrumental in bringing about his death. So it is most unlikely that either Jesus or the early church would have wanted a ministerial priesthood based in any way on the Jewish model. After the destruction of the temple in Jerusalem in 70 AD the Jewish priesthood ceased to exist, because their only function was to serve the temple. When this happened the new Christian communities gradually began to think in terms of priesthood. Priesthood developed slowly over the next hundred years or so, gradually subsuming the variety of ministries into one person and role, the priest. He became the leader of the community, the presider at the Eucharist, and the one in whom all ministries were combined. I am sure that this development made for better and easier organisation, and more centralised control, but it is hard not to regret that it happened. Undoubtedly the variety of ministries, and the involvement of the community as a whole, suffered as a consequence. It was a good bit later, not until the twelfth century, that celibacy became a compulsory part of priesthood.

It surprises me that, in spite of the widely accepted understanding of how the early communities developed, it is still regularly stated by church spokesmen that Jesus instituted the priesthood. Recently the spokesman for the Irish Bishops' Conference, in response to a call from a priest for a review of ministry within the church, stated the following: 'The church received the priesthood from Christ, it did not create it. To presume to change the priesthood of Christ is to deny the authority of Christ'.

As far as I can understand the thinking behind statements like this, it seems to suggest that when Jesus commissioned the apostles to go out and preach the good news he was actually ordaining them to priestly ministry. That is surely stretching the meaning of the event beyond what can reasonably be done. The most that can be said about the type of statement made by the bishop's spokesman is that it is an arguable position. It has no clear support in the New Testament. And there is a great deal to indicate the opposite. I believe it is no longer valid for the church authority to proclaim as essential dogma something that is seriously debated by the scholars. A quote from Raymond Brown, the acknowledged expert on New Testament scholarship, is useful here. This is from *Biblical Reflections on Crises Facing the Church*, which was published in 1975:

From the New Testament it appears that the clear conceptualisation of the Christian priesthood came only after the destruction of the Jerusalem temple in 70 AD. When the Jewish priesthood no longer offered sacrifice in the temple, Christians came to see more clearly that their Eucharistic meal was the Christian sacrifice and that those who presided at it could be called priests. But the question of who would serve as priests was still in flux ... while prophets were permitted to celebrate the Eucharist, the role of a more regular clergy was encouraged. Eventually the practice of a public ordination by a bishop was seen to fit best the needs of the church.

Brown then goes on to make a point which is relevant to a number of the arguments I am making in this book:

In such a reconstruction of the origins of priesthood, obviously history and sociology entered in: the way the church structured its ministry was affected by its life situation. If this is so, why cannot the history and sociology of our time guide the church to a different procedure and a different set of candidates? If church needs can be better met by the ordination of women, why not introduce the practice?

One of the disturbing aspects about the church today is that when the authorities come out with statements similar to the one quoted above asserting that Christ gave the priesthood to the church and that as a consequence it cannot be changed, the Scripture scholars of today, who know perfectly well that these types of statements have little if any basis in biblical writing, remain quiet. They do not open their mouths. It is one of the sad facts of our church that, when Raymond Brown was writing in the 1970s, it was easier for a scholar to give his or her opinion, where it differed from the official position, than it is today. Most of today's Scripture scholars are lecturers or professors in Catholic seminaries or universities. If they publicly contradicted an official church position, they would quickly find themselves out of a job.

The position I am arguing in this book is that modern scholarship indicates that neither the particular structures of government that we have within the church today, nor the current forms of ministry, can claim to have any specific divine origin. They can claim it in a general sense, but not down to the detail of how it is put into practice. So we need to allow this very important debate about ministry to continue within the church. Believing that the exact type of priesthood we have today in the church is exactly as Christ wanted has blocked very necessary reforms and changes. When we free ourselves from the burden of divine choice then we can begin to openly discuss whether a particular system or structure is what will serve the church best at this particular time.

I have said elsewhere in this book that the period around the twelfth century was particularly significant in shaping the type of church that now exists. It was the era of Gregory VII and Innocent III, the two big figures in the centralising of church authority in Rome, and setting up the bishop of Rome as the ultimate authority, greater than any other bishop, and even greater than a church council. The same process that occurred to ministry in the first two centuries happened in the church generally around this time. Authority and control was subsumed from the different regions, and put into the hands of one person, the pope. It seems to me a tragedy that this happened both to priesthood and to the church at large. The church, which began by very much working on the model of community, with shared authority and shared ministry, became increasingly centralised and autocratic.

Problems with the Present System
I believe it is now time for a serious look at ministry within the church, and a rethinking of how it should be structured for the good of the church in the future. First I will outline the problems with the present system.

• The meaning and practice of ministry has been narrowed down, and has lost a lot of its richness by being focused on one person within the community. The priest has become far too important, and has taken too much on himself. We need again to separate different ministries. And when we do that it is important that any one ministry not be seen as more important than another. Only in this way can we begin to rediscover that form of community of the early church.

• Priests, because all ministries were in their hands, became much too powerful within the community. Power is possibly the most corrupting influence on human nature, and priests have tended to lord it over the people. They became major authority figures, with positions of great status and importance. As this developed it was inevitable that the original notion of ministry as service to the community tended to become lost. Instead of servants, the priests became bosses, authority figures, who laid down the law. Also, because of their position as leaders of the Eucharist, and because of the way the Eucharistic celebration had developed over the centuries, the priest took on an almost superhuman mystique. It was he who celebrated the Eucharist, up high on an altar, with his back to the people. It had become an almost magic ritual, which the people attended but in which they did not participate in any real sense of the word. People actually began to believe that it was the priest, with his 'sacred hands' who changed the bread and wine into the body and blood of Christ. The church encouraged this misunderstanding because it gave an elevated status to the priest. But it was wrong. The role of the priest is much simpler. As the member of the community chosen to preside at the Eucharist, on behalf of the community he calls on the Spirit to come and perform this wonderful work. 'Let your Spirit come upon these gifts to make them holy, so that they may become the body and blood of Our Lord Jesus Christ.'

• The priest as celibate also contributed to the development of this mystique. He was removed from the ordinary life of the people, living often in a large remote house, and not really mixing with people. They tended to see him as special, holier than everyone else. The theology of priesthood that was taught at the time added to this. It emphasised the power of the priest in changing the bread and wine at mass, and the holiness of the priest's hands. All of this was a long way from the original idea of the Eucharist being the celebration of the whole community of faith. In setting the priest up as special and holy, it laid the ground for all the shock and horror that greeted the revelations of sexual deviation by priests in our time.

• Because power and decision-making became centralised in the hands of the priest, the ordinary believer became powerless. He or she was no longer a real member of a community of believers, but rather more like a consumer of the religion that was handed down from on high. This had a seriously negative effect on the church generally. It turned the people into passive receivers, and after years of this it is now very difficult to get people to begin to take responsibility again. This coincided with a major increase in the devotional side of religion. Saints, shrines, miracles, novenas and all the other trappings of devotional religion began to take over. Religion became more emotional and less reflective. It became in some ways a consumer product that the priests provided for the people. And it did serve to keep people in their place.

• The fact that for many centuries, almost down to our own time, priests were generally more educated than the people put them in an extra position of power. They came to be seen, not just as the holiest person in the community, but also the most knowledgeable. And knowledge is power. The fact that this has changed in the western world, and that now almost everyone is educated, has been a big factor in lessening the perceived status of the priest.

• As a result of most of the points already made, particularly the centralising of power in the hands of the priest and the rule of celibacy, priests gradually developed into a separate elite group or caste, and so we have the existence of what we call clericalism. By this we mean an enclosed group from a particular profession, who tend to keep to themselves, speak their own language, and are not really open to influence or opinion from outside the group. When I was in the seminary, and during my early years as a priest, I was encouraged to mix with other priests. It was a good thing to do, I was informed. I should meet with them for prayer, to discuss the scriptures, to socialise, and I should go on holidays with other priests. Part of the reason for this was the vow of celibacy. It was considered not very safe to do any of the above with a woman, particularly the socialising or the holidays, because it would inevitably lead to temptations against celibacy. The good priest was the one who stayed within his own group. He met the ordinary people as he went about his work; he ministered to them and performed the rituals of the church for them. But when it came to meeting his human needs this was to be done within his own set, with other priests. Within this set the priest is confirmed in his way of thinking. He develops a particular style of language and behaviour. He becomes comfortable in the lifestyle, with all the privileges and status that go with it. And he is increasingly removed from the people to whom he ministers. This is the almost inevitable result of any close-knit and exclusive group. He is supported in his position of power and status by other members of his group. The absence of a female presence and voice in the group leaves it open to becoming even more closed and 'laddish' and immature. While other professions might have good reason for developing their particular close-knit group, with its own language and culture, for priests the clerical caste system has been, in my view, an almost totally negative development.

Necessary Reforms

I think it is obvious from all the happenings of recent years that the priesthood as we know it is no longer serving the church well. To put it simply, it is just not working. It is in urgent need of reform. I will list the reforms that are necessary, as I see them:

• A return to the Gospel notion of ministry as service. This is absolutely fundamental. It is hard to see how the present-day priesthood, with centuries of power and status behind it, can really change to the extent needed in this regard. This is not to suggest that all priests are power-hungry control freaks. Quite the contrary. There are many remarkable priests who really do serve the people, and who live lives of great dedication and commitment. But even they are damaged and their work is compromised by the system within which they operate. In order to rediscover the notion of service as Jesus intended, we need to dismantle much of the present system of ministry.

• A return to the early church notion of the separation of ministries. This is as equally crucial a reform as the first one. It would draw many more people into ministry, and help to recreate the spirit of community in the church. It would remove the mystique around the position of priest, and power and responsibility would be shared, for the greater good of all.

• Compulsory celibacy needs to be abolished. I have written more fully about this in another part of the book. Suffice to say here that it has been one of the big influences in creating the exclusive caste system of clericalism that priests inhabit. Marriage and family would do wonders in bringing priests back into ordinary life, and making them equal members of the believing community.

• It is intolerable to have a situation where many parishes and communities are deprived of the Eucharist because of church rules about priesthood. It is a perfect example of how an institution regards its own laws and structures as being of more importance than the people whose service is the whole *raison d'être* of its existence. It would be a small change, and quickly accepted by the large majority of the faithful, for the church to begin to ordain married men. In most of the numerous parishes in which I have worked I have seen suitable candidates, men who are living good lives and who are committed to the community and the church. They could assume the position of presiding at the Eucharist with some training, though not necessarily the long seminary course now proscribed for priests. This move could also coincide with a welcome back into ministry for all those priests who left the ministry over the years in order to get married, but who still wish to exercise their priesthood. It is an extraordinary anomaly that Church of England and Episcopalian priests can convert to Catholicism and practise as Catholic priests while remaining married, while Catholic priests who got married are not allowed practise.

• The question of the ordination of women should be open for discussion within the church without fear of sanctions from the authorities. The argument that Jesus did not ordain women should never again be heard, and the issue should be recognised for what it is, a matter of church discipline. Change might need to come more slowly in this area, and a great deal of education would be needed. But other churches have shown that it is possible, and that after a while it becomes accepted by the large majority of the believers. The fact that a small, hard-core minority might not accept it and might leave the church is not a reason for not doing something that is right.

I will finish with another quote from Raymond Brown, this time from his book *The Churches the Apostles Left Behind*:

There is a special problem in churches that have an ordained priesthood in their church structure. The presence of an ordained priesthood can have the unfortunate side effect of minimalising an appreciation of the priesthood of all believers. In relation to the equality of Christians as disciples, it is especially difficult for the ordained priesthood to be kept in the category of service to God and the community, for the ordained will frequently be assumed to be more important and automatically more holy. Because ordination is seen as a sacrament and priests deal with sacred things, they are frequently regarded as better than ordinary Christians. In my own church some would find surprising this almost elementary affirmation: the day when a person is baptised is more important than the day when a person is ordained priest or bishop. The first sacrament, after all, touches on salvation; it constitutes one a child of God, a dignity that goes beyond designation to the special service of God.

Ministry is of vital importance to the church. The present system is not working. I have given my views on what needs to be done. I believe that these are the issues that we could and should be discussing, that we urgently need to discuss.

VIII

THE DECLINE OF RELIGIOUS LIFE
IN THE CHURCH

Religious orders and congregations have been at the centre of the life and success of the Catholic church almost from the beginning. At various times they have been compared to the specialist units in armies, specifically trained for particular tasks. Down through the centuries they have taken many different forms. In the earliest centuries of the life of the church they were largely contemplative, meaning that their lives were lived around prayer, contemplation and manual labour, the work being usually farming or one or other of the crafts. Indeed manual labour was a strong feature of their lives, at which they spent many hours each day. For that reason some of these monasteries gradually became very wealthy and owned large tracts of the most fertile land. This caused great problems through the centuries, leading to a lot of corruption in monastic life and to conflict with the civil authorities. Greed for money and possession can corrupt within a monastery as elsewhere. As regards the lifestyle, apart from those who chose the way of the hermit, living alone in some remote place, community living was the norm in these monastic settlements. Strict silence was observed for long periods each day.

This monastic way of living religious life, which began with men, but quickly developed communities of women, has been the most successful and enduring form of religious life in the history of the church. I believe that the reason for its long survival and success was that its purpose was clear. The monks devoted their lives to contemplation of the meaning of life and the mystery of the Divine Being. As such they were touching on something so fundamental that it would inevitably appeal to people of all times and ages.

Apostolic Religious Life

Many hundreds of years later, during the period we call the Middle Ages, a different style of religious life developed, which is commonly referred to as apostolic religious life. While this form was also usually lived out in monasteries or convents, it had a more diverse focus. Apostolic religious communities were founded to do a particular work. The Jesuits, for instance, were to be in the forefront of the intellectual life of the church, among other things they were to set up schools to educate the sons of the ruling classes. The Dominicans were to devote themselves to preaching. Various orders of sisters and brothers were founded to educate the children of the poor, or to nurse the sick. People like Nano Nagle and Edmund Ignatius Rice are outstanding examples in our own country. What made this form of religious life more problematic was that it had two different, and to some extent contradictory aims. Because the way of monastic life had been established for centuries, and a rule of life had been clearly laid out for it, the new orders also adopted this rule, with only minor variations to allow for the different life style involved in their apostolates. When I joined the Redemptorists, who are a good illustration of an order living what we call apostolic religious life, I was told that we must be Carthusians at home and apostles abroad. (The Carthusians are an order of strict contemplatives.) What was meant was that when we were at home we must live in our monasteries as contemplatives, but be willing also to go out into the world in the exercise of our particular work, which in our case was to be extraordinary preachers of the Word of God to the poor.

This style of apostolic religious life thrived for hundreds of years, and each century saw the foundation of new institutes with new goals, depending on the needs of the time. It probably experienced its greatest flowering from the mid-eighteenth to the mid-twentieth century. When I joined over forty years ago monasteries and convents in many parts of the world were bursting at the seams, and were busily erecting new buildings to cope with this influx. I belong to a family of four, all of whom entered religious life. This may sound very strange now, but in that era it was not particularly unusual. Half a century ago prosperity hadn't yet come to this little island, and for the great majority of the population life was poor and simple. I think it is worth commenting a little on that period in Ireland, and on the reasons why such an enormous number of young Irish men and women were becoming priests or religious, because something similar is happening now in other countries in the developing world.

Dominance of Church Influence
The most significant feature of this period of Irish life was that the Catholic church was by far the most dominant influence on society at large. Consequently there was a coherence about life and about what we believed as individuals and as society, which is markedly absent today. Into this coherent belief system, both the theology of the church and the generally accepted philosophy of the people fitted perfectly. Religious life made sense within it. It is ironic that while religious life was meant to be a contrary statement, a concrete expression of values and lifestyle very different to those accepted by society at large, in fact it was the opposite. To become a priest and religious meant for us a major step up the social ladder, leading to honour, respect and probably a more comfortable life than we might otherwise have. Since practically everyone was Catholic, went to mass regularly, and gave at least nominal consent to its teachings, our way of life fitted comfortably into the belief system of the time. The outstanding features of that belief system were as follows:

• That this life was but a brief preparation for an infinitely more important existence, eternal life.

• That in fact this life was not of any great importance in itself except to live it in such a way that you would assure yourself of salvation. Since salvation was attained chiefly by avoiding serious sin, the sinless life was the one to aspire to.

• The great sin at the time, and the one that most endangered your salvation because almost all transgressions were in the serious category, was sexual sin. The best way of avoiding the dangers in this area was to have nothing at all to do with sex. The obvious way to do that was to live a celibate life.

• Religious life was seen as a higher state of holiness than any other form of life. It was definitely considered to be a higher category than marriage, which traditionally had been viewed as a reluctant concession for those who could not avoid what was called concupiscence.

• Service of others was held up as an important value. We were encouraged to think of others before ourselves. To give our lives completely in the service of others was the greatest thing of all. We believed that was what we were doing when we entered religious life.

It is obvious from all of this that Catholic beliefs and practice had come to dominate over every other way of looking at life. Of course this could only happen in a closed and fairly primitive society. The ease of communication in modern life has made that type of situation impossible, at least in the developed world, and increasingly also in other areas.

Apart from the spiritual gains that went with living the religious life, there were also more immediate temporal rewards. Religious were highly thought of by people generally, and were given a position of considerable status and influence in society. This was highly significant. By joining religious life a person could climb many steps of the social ladder. In the society at that time religious life was one of the few ways that a person could get access to third level education, and be given a chance to travel the world. All of this, of course, has totally changed here, where there are now endless opportunities for young people, and where priests and religious have lost most of their former status due to a decline in faith and the scandals in the church. But the situation that I describe from the Ireland of the 1950s would appear to be replicated in some African and other developing societies today where large numbers are now entering religious life and becoming priests.

Ageing Communities

I and my contemporaries in religious life have lived to see ageing communities, monasteries and convents being closed down and sold off, and few if any new recruits. This has happened in such an extraordinarily short time that it is hard to understand or integrate. All the indications are that this form of life is in terminal decline in the western world. We are quickly reaching the stage where renewal will be impossible. When I first wrote about this over ten years ago I suggested that it was only the apostolic religious orders that were dying out, and that the contemplative ones would survive. I proposed that the reason for this was the difference in focus between the two. Apostolic religious orders, because they tried to combine the two forms of life, contemplative and active, had never really developed a clear enough focus to help them survive the crisis brought on both by the modern world and the Second Vatican Council. Contemplative orders, on the other hand, had a clear aim, the search for meaning and for God, and it was an aim that was so fundamental to humanity that it would survive any upheaval. Now I am not so sure. The information I am getting would suggest that even contemplative religious life would seem to be suffering greatly, particularly in Europe. The decline came a little later than it came to the apostolic groups. But the same pattern is emerging.

Stagnation

Religious life had become stagnated during the nineteenth and the first half of the twentieth century. It is ironic that what appeared to be the time of greatest flourishing, if one judges by numbers joining, can now be seen to be the time when what really flourished were the seeds of decay. This of course was also an era of great stagnation in the church generally, as I have written elsewhere in this book. The way the stagnation manifested itself in religious life was in the development of rigid structures and controls. Rules of life became extraordinarily detailed, until almost every moment of a person's day was directed from above. From the moment the religious got up in the morning to when he or she lay down to sleep, life was controlled by the rule. The superior was all powerful. His or her word was law, and was to be seen as the will of God. The bell, which rang many times each day calling us to the various activities, was to be heard as the voice of God. A gradual shift had taken place, probably unnoticed by the people of the time, which I believe was crucial to the ultimate decline. Orders and congregations, which were originally founded to serve some need in society or the church, began to turn in on themselves. Because the life was so rigid, and the rule was regarded as sacred, the energy of the group was directed inward to the correct living of this life rather than outward to the work that was the original inspiration. Because obedience was seen as the primary virtue, external observance of the law was the way in which goodness was assessed. People were judged by how well they observed the rule rather than their commitment to the work of the congregation. They were discouraged from thinking for themselves. In fact, thinking for oneself was regarded as sinful and anathema to the religious. What was the need for thinking for

oneself when God spoke through the superior? Most of the religious orders were founded by people of great originality and
vision, of energy and creativity. They developed into institutions
which did their best to stifle all these qualities in their members.

Failure to Adjust to Council Teaching

It is ironic that it was the Second Vatican Council that accelerated the decline of this form of religious life. Apart from the
documents that were produced, the fact that the council happened at all was immensely significant. To have the bishops and
leaders of the church gathered in intense dialogue and discussion
on all aspects of the faith changed the whole atmosphere. We had
grown accustomed to a church that was dogmatic, provided answers and pre-empted discussion. Now we were witnessing a church
that questioned, discussed and gave permission to people to think
for themselves and find new answers, even a variety of different
answers. As regards the documents, it wasn't so much 'Perfectae
Caritatis', the document on religious life itself, which made a difference. That one was quite traditional. It was the 'Pastoral Con-
stitution on the Church in the Modern World' that set us alight:

> It is, however, only in freedom that man can turn himself towards
> what is good. The people of our time prize freedom very highly and
> strive eagerly for it. In this they are right.

It is hard for us today to appreciate the significance of sentences
like this one, and the impact they made on religious life at the
time. Thinking, use of the intellect, having freedom, taking personal responsibility, were now being encouraged, even praised.
They cut the ground from under the traditional form of religious
life. They destroyed the underlying philosophy and spirituality on
which it was based. Unless religious life had the ability to change
radically, and to adapt its structures to a very new reality, it could

not survive. But religious life had become so stagnant in that era that it was particularly unsuited to the challenge to change and adapt. It was rigid and inflexible – it had solidified.

The council also challenged the notion that religious life was a specially privileged life, with a surer guarantee of salvation. This had been central to the success of the old days. It was a nice feeling to know that your way of life was special, and to believe that it was a more spiritual life than any other. That gave a person motivation to endure the deprivations of the life. It seemed a small enough thing to give up the joys of sex and marriage, joys which were denigrated and restricted by the theology of the time in any case, for the almost guarantee of a high place in Heaven. But the council said that 'all Christians, in any state or walk of life, are called to the fullness of Christian life and to the perfection of love'. If one could achieve holiness in any walk of life, why then give up so much to enter religious life?

The council emphasised the dignity and beauty of married love. Marriage was no longer a necessary evil in order to propagate the human race and control sexual desire. Marriage was declared by the council to be a holy state. Sex was good. As the council documents say:

> Married love is uniquely expressed and perfected by the exercise of the acts proper to marriage. Hence the acts in marriage by which the intimate and chaste union of the spouses takes place are noble and honourable.

The language is cumbersome, but the message is clear. The church has declared the sexual act noble and honourable. Again it is hard for a modern person to appreciate the significance of this. Fifteen hundred years of church teaching were in fact being reversed, even though theologians tried to present it as a development rather than a change. From this moment on, celibacy was going to be more difficult. It is easier to convince yourself of the value of abstaining from something that was generally regarded as an occasion of sin and a serious danger to salvation rather than something that had become noble and honourable.

The will of the superior had been presented as the voice of God. But the council talked about the dignity of each human person, the importance of developing the intellect, and the need for dialogue. From the moment dialogue was introduced, the power of the superior rapidly eroded. A new system of authority, based on the community in dialogue, began to be attempted. This turned out to be extremely difficult, particularly for people who had no experience of having personal views or making personal decisions.

With so much prominence given by the council to the notions of freedom and dialogue, obviously obedience would never be the same again. Soon people began to assert that obedience was due, not to the superior, but to the community and one's own conscience. The old clarity of command had dissipated, and the structures began rapidly to break down. Uniformity could no longer be imposed, and it began to be replaced by its opposite, individuality. This had a serious impact on community living.

Time of Great Debate

When religious life became stagnated in the nineteenth and early twentieth centuries peripheral things had assumed great importance. Because obedience was the primary virtue, external observance of the law was the way in which goodness was assessed. The small details of the law were writ large. Following the Second Vatican Council the initial battles were fought over the structures of community living. Things like the daily timetable, the format of community prayer, whether everyone had to attend community prayer together, and probably most of all the observance of the night curfew, became major bones of contention. As the laws began to be flouted, superiors found themselves with less authority to exercise the traditional sanctions. During all those years the debate within religious life waged at two levels. Firstly, there was an immense intellectual and theological debate, sparked off by the council, and fuelled by new theological and scriptural writings. These covered all aspects of the human and Christian life. The debate was carried on with a relish brought about by the centuries of stagnation, and the new found freedom of speech. Secondly, within communities, there was another debate, of considerably less intellectual weight, but by no means less intense, over the small issues of community living. Some people saw issues like the time at which a religious should be home at night as of major importance. Maybe they were right, in the sense that these were the things that had been elevated to this level, and it was on the observance of such rules that the whole house of cards had come to be built and eventually collapsed.

Of course it wasn't only the Vatican Council that took the ground from under religious life. All of this was happening within the context of a rapidly changing world. The communications revolution had arrived, so that it was no longer possible to hide people away in monasteries and convents immune from the whirlwind of ideas going on outside. The old values of religious life, based on obedient acceptance rather than reflective personal commitment, were being challenged on all sides. Suffice to say that a decline set in which has accelerated to the stage we are in now, where there is little sign of a future for this form of religious life in the western world.

Because I am part of an ageing religious community I have become acutely aware in the past few years how an institution that is not attracting new blood ages more rapidly and dramatically than I would have anticipated. It seems that as the average age of a group passes the mid-fifties the level of disintegration multiplies by the year. Some of the people, who are still regarded as young relative to the group in general, die before their time, maybe of heart attacks or brain tumours, with cancer taking its inevitable toll. As the number of active people declines and the burden of the work falls on fewer members, the unexpected death of even one key member can be devastating. An older age group also tends to have a higher ratio of mental and emotional sickness, of depression and various anxiety-related illnesses. The cumulative result is that in the western world most religious communities are inhabited increasingly by old and sick members.

Weak Leadership

Just as in the church in general, the standard of leadership within religious life has become more critical than might have been expected. Positions of leadership in religious life are often occupied by women or men who have neither the health, the energy nor the ability to do the job. This of course is partly a result of the trends I have highlighted above, but I also think there is another reason. Over the last forty years I have seen a great many people, both male and female, depart the religious life. They have left at various stages, some in their formation years, and others having given a great part of their lives to their institute. The official position is that those of us who have stayed are the faithful ones, that we are the ones who have continued to live the life of dedication and commitment. But I wonder if that is true. Maybe it is the case that the ones who left were the talented ones, the ones with imagination and initiative, the clear-sighted ones who could see what was coming. Is that part of the reason why we in religious life, and indeed the church in general, are suffering from poor leadership?

New Recruits

The problem of new recruits to religious life has been a particularly difficult one. I have been suggesting for some time that we should not take any more applicants because we have nothing further to offer them. Both our age structure and the declining quality of our community living and our work mean that it is no longer advisable for young people to attach themselves to us. Some religious groups have indeed been following this policy, but most have continued actively to seek new members. Along with the difficulty of attracting them in the first place has been the problem of retaining them. The fall-out has been great, and the few who have continued on to final profession or ordination often find it hard to fit into the traditional lifestyle and apostolate of the congregation they joined. They can end up doing their own thing, and having only a tenuous connection to their institute. This is very understandable in the circumstances, but it is difficult to see how a future for the particular congregation can be built around these few young members. I believe that the time has come when we need to face the fact that we should not take any more young people into our way of life. Why invite young people into a way of life that is so obviously declining? Surely it is placing an impossible burden on them. This is the most difficult and painful question for any institution to have to face. Its natural instinct is to preserve itself, and the members within it need the assurance that there will be a future to give meaning to their own lives. Who wants to see the way of life, which they have believed in and given themselves to so completely, die out with them? There is also the natural desire to have someone coming along to look after you in your old age, and to carry on your traditions and charism. If our generation of religious give up on the possibility of a future, and stop taking recruits, then we face certain extinction. How would it be possible for us to preserve any sort of morale among ourselves? Even to begin to ask the question about whether we are entitled to take any more new members is in itself a blow to morale, and could so easily become a self-fulfilling prophecy. And yet, not to ask it is to fly in the face of an ever more obvious reality.

Some among us argue that while religious life is in serious decline, it is not terminal. They suggest that this way of life will survive, with much smaller numbers and in a somewhat different form from what we have known. Consequently they argue for the continued acceptance of new members, because it will be they, with help and support from existing members, who will shape the new future. By closing our doors to new members, they assert, we lose hope in a very real future, and we betray the style of life to which we are committed.

I don't accept this reading of the situation. I agree that something new will surely develop, but I don't think that it is the necessary pattern of life that the new comes from the embers of the old. I believe that what is old and tired has to die, and that new growth will come from other sources, maybe very surprising ones. The tired old earth needs rest; it needs the fallow period in order to renew itself. Then it must be ploughed, harrowed and manured, so that a renewed earth can be ready to receive the new seed, and the new roots can go deep into the soil. The desperate clinging to life of the old can be an obstacle to new growth. The weeds of the past need to be cleared away with the harrow in order to make space for the spring crop.

This issue is of intense concern not just to religious, but to the church in general. Without the specialist forces of committed religious the evangelical thrust of the church would be greatly weakened. It was mainly religious who in the past set out to foreign countries without any thought for themselves and spread the Christian message. Their lack of human ties and their vow of obedience meant that they were available to go where they were sent. Without them the work of the church would be seriously depleted. If they die out, as now seems likely, what will replace them?

Suggestions for the Future

I will attempt to give some outlines of how a new style of religious life might be different to what we have known. Even though the three vows of poverty, chastity and obedience have been at the centre of religious life from the beginning of the church, I believe that the changes we have experienced are so dramatic that the time has come to take a new look at them.

The first thing I would suggest is that it is time to free dedicated religious living from the burden of compulsory celibacy. I have written about compulsory celibacy in relation to priesthood in another part of this book, commenting on the major changes that have taken place in the understanding of the human body, marriage and the essential meaning of the sexual relationship. I have also spelled out some of the unfortunate attitudes to sexuality and women that have been part of the history of the church, and that have undoubtedly influenced its teaching. The recent exposure of the extent of sexual abuse among priests and religious has had the effect of raising questions about celibacy as a way of life. One of the lessons we have got to learn is that in future celibacy must never have a compulsory tag attached to it. No form of life, even religious life, should have celibacy as a *sine qua non*. Future commitment to celibacy has to be clearly seen as a voluntary choice, freely made by the individual, and not part of an overall package. Only in this way will its credibility as a way of life be restored.

I also believe that new forms of religious life need to rethink the vow of obedience. Obedience is an important virtue, and it plays a part in developing a rounded Christian life. But when it is taken as a vow of life by a group of men or women it can assume other, less worthy, characteristics. There is no doubt that it was often used in religious life in the past as a method of control and manipulation. The idea that a person should completely submit their will and beliefs to those of the superior, as we were taught to do in our early religious training, is too reminiscent of Nazi Germany and the worst forms of communism. I am old enough to remember religious superiors who governed in the name of the vow of obedience, but who acted in ways that were anything but Christian. Obedience is a dangerous virtue in the hands of large institutions who like to keep their subjects under control for the good of the institution. Its misuse, as I have pointed out, has been one of the big reasons for the collapse of the whole system. Whatever form of obedience is exercised in the religious life of the future, it should never be in the hands of one individual, but should be expressed in some way through the will of the whole group.

The other traditional concept that needs to be rethought is lifelong commitment as an essential part of religious dedication. Certainly there will always be a place for this, but equally there should be an option of temporary commitment. People should be allowed to give themselves to the form of life for a period of time, make their contribution, and move on.

What of the last of the traditional vows, poverty? This is the most solidly based of the three vows in the teaching of Christ, and it will surely play an important part in a future form of religious life, but it too needs to be understood differently from the past. Christian teaching seems to me to prize detachment, as distinct from poverty. Indeed poverty in itself is not something to be prized, but to be eradicated where possible. Maybe the central bond between people who are attempting to live a dedicated religious life in the future will be the notion of detachment. In a world that is increasingly materialistic, where people's energy is often focused almost exclusively on acquiring money and success and all that goes with them, probably the essential witness that a Christian community can give is detachment. A group of people who commit themselves to living by different values, who do not devote more of their energy than is necessary to material things, who do not wish to acquire more than they need, but who attempt to proclaim in their way of life that love is the fundamental value, would proclaim the Christian message very powerfully. If these people were not shut away in large buildings, living lives that appear strange and unreal, but were rather part of the ordinary world, their witness would be all the more effective. They would consist of people from different walks and ways of life, male and female, married and single, from the different sections of society. Structures could be put in place that would enable them to come together on a regular basis to support each other, to pray and to celebrate the Christian rituals. There might even be a core group who would live in a more detached way, somewhat similar to our present forms, and these could conceivably make a commitment to celibacy and to lifelong perseverance if they wished. But it would be very important that they would not be seen as superior to the others. Different classes within the same institute bedevilled religious life in the past.

I know that there are some new styles of religious living beginning to emerge, in Paris and elsewhere, somewhat along the lines I have outlined. But it is hard for our generation to know how all this might develop. It is for a new generation to shape what is needed for the future. Our task is not to be an obstacle, not to block the coming into being of the new. We may be able to help by sharing our experience of what was good and bad in our life. But if we desperately try to cling to what is no longer viable we are in danger of hindering rather than assisting the work of the Spirit of God.

IX

CURRENT ISSUES

There is a priest working in a city parish in Ireland. He has spent more than twenty years in the parish, and is now well into his seventies. The parish has a population of about 10,000 Catholics. At first he had the assistance of two other priests, but in recent years that was reduced to one. He wasn't blessed with good luck, in that the two most active and skilled curates who worked with him over the years both left the priesthood. At this stage there is no young man available in the diocese, so he depends on help from men of his own age who have retired after years working on the foreign missions. These are good, dedicated men, but due to age and ill health their contribution is limited.

This parish priest is an approachable man and has a natural, easy rapport with people. He works hard. When, some years ago, a young curate wanted a day off each week, he looked at him with amazement. This was a new concept to him. But he readily agreed, knowing that the new generation had different needs that must be met. For himself he slips out maybe one or two evenings a week to the local golf course and plays a game with some of his friends. He isn't an avid reader of theology, but he does his best to keep in touch, and he believes deeply in the concept of church as community of the believers.

When I gave a mission in his parish I was struck by the fact that the sacristy of the church was a place where people congregated freely. He had all the usual structures of involvement, a pastoral council, a liturgy group, ministers of the Word and Eucharist, etc. But his gift was that he drew these people in, so that they did not see themselves as doing a particular job for the church, but as part of the whole apostolic effort. They were interested and concerned about every aspect of the life of the local church, and they wanted to help out in any way they could. When I commented on this, and complimented him on the wonderful group of people he had gathered around him, and the general air of friendliness and cooperation, he made the simple point that no other approach was possible, that it would be impossible for him to run the parish without their help. 'With our seminaries nearly empty, all the indications are that in a few years' time there will be no resident priest in this parish. When that time comes my hope is that these people will be the nucleus that will keep the community of believers alive, and preserve the faith.'

I thought of that man, and his vibrant group of helpers, some months later when the Vatican once again drew up restrictions on the use of lay ministers of the Eucharist. They were to be called on only in case of necessity, where there was no priest available. I hoped that his people would not read this document. They would inevitably experience it as a rebuff, telling them they were not really part of the church, that their help was only required when someone better was not present. The effect would be to make them feel not wanted at a time when they are wanted more than ever before, at a time when we, the clergy, should be down on our knees thanking God that such people exist.

The Future of Ministry is a Burning Issue
It is now very clear that the church in the western world is not going to continue to provide priests to minister to the people in the foreseeable future. Despite some small indications of an increase in vocations to more traditional orders there is no sign of any substantial upsurge of vocations to the priesthood. That leaves the church with a fairly simple and dramatic choice. It can do

one of two things. There are places in the world where seminaries are bursting at the seams, and where more priests are being ordained than will be needed for the local churches. This is happening mostly in Africa and parts of the Far East and South America. Priests can be brought in from these countries to minister to churches in Europe and elsewhere. A friend in Canada tells me that this is already happening there, that a great number of priests are coming in from Africa and the Far East and staffing their parishes. It is beginning to happen in Europe, but not yet to any great degree in Ireland. It will undoubtedly be problematic, though I suppose there is something ironically appropriate about priests from the developing world coming to the west, and bringing their cultural baggage mixed up with the message, when for centuries we westerners imposed our culture on them under the guise of Christianity. I am not talking about the situation where priests come with some of the migrant groups that are arriving here from places like Nigeria and Brazil. It is when they come to serve in local Irish parishes that the problem of cultural difference will arise. Before they come they will need to be carefully instructed both in the culture and in the style of church that is prevalent here.

This solution to the ministry problem is the one currently favoured by the authorities in Rome. Recently a high level meeting of bishops from Europe and Africa took place to begin planning for large numbers of African priests to come to Europe.

The other solution to the problem of declining numbers of priests in the west would be to begin to redefine the understanding of ministry in the church, as I have suggested in the previous chapter. It is not simply a matter of opening up the priesthood to married men and women. By doing that we would be retaining the present system, with all its culture of clerical control and domination, and merely widening its reach. With women in particular sharing in priestly ministry, it would be less of a closed shop.

But I believe something more than that is needed. And that is why I suggest in this book that we return to the early church understanding of ministry, dividing up the functions of the present day priest among the different members of the community, and in that way making more use of the gifts and talents that are available. A Christian community that would be served by the people themselves would be a very different reality to one where a minister is brought in from outside, particularly with a different culture and understanding of church and faith.

The Vatican prefers to retain our present system of priesthood because it is easier to control. I suppose when they are at the centre of power, and have exercised it for centuries, they cannot conceive of a church without their dominant position. Maybe the future is with them.

In his 'Letter from Rome' of 3 December 2004, John L. Allen, Jr., a reporter for the *National Catholic Reporter* who posts an article on the internet each week under the above title, writes about how the balance is shifting in the church from the north to the south, both in terms of numbers and vitality:

> The south is where Catholicism is growing, and there is a remarkable vitality and self-confidence about the church in the developing world. Priests from the developing world will be arriving in growing numbers in Europe and the United States.

He then goes on to draw some conclusion as to what he believes this will mean for the church of the future:

> It may push social issues higher on the church's radar screen, since underdevelopment, HIV/AIDS, systemic corruption and the development of civil society are pastoral urgencies facing bishops from the south.
>   On the other hand it could mean that some long-standing concerns in the west will increasingly occupy a back burner, such as

gender equity in the church, the deconstruction of clericalism and debates over sexual morality. Further, the tendency is towards conservative stances on issues such as homosexuality, as witnessed by the current crisis in the Anglican Communion.

I hope his analysis is not correct.

I recently visited an old and ailing priest in a nursing home. He was asking me about my life and work, and gradually the conversation widened to cover the general state of the church, with declining congregations and only a tiny number of vocations to the priesthood. Either through old age or the amount of medication he was taking, the poor man's voice was slightly indistinct. But the following sentence emerged clearly and distinctly.

'The big question for us is what is God saying to us in all of this?'

He had introduced a new level to our conversation, and I sat in silence for a moment. I almost missed the next sentence, he spoke it so quietly.

'And how can we hear what God is saying?'

One of the main points I am making in this book is that the Vatican structure is not receptive to the voice of the Spirit; that it is almost incapable of hearing that wind 'which blows where it will', but gently. The Vatican cannot hear because in its subconscious it is afraid of becoming extinct if the power goes back to the local communities. A radical change, a conversion in the full sense of that word, is needed to make the Vatican capable of listening and receiving the voice of the Spirit. What is needed is a big change in the system and exercise of authority in the Catholic church.

New Answers Needed

Recently a religious community gathered for a day of recollection. Typical of the situation in religious life today, of the fourteen who sat around the youngest was almost sixty, and most of them were between seventy-five and eighty-five. The preacher for the day, also in his seventies, spoke about the religious vows and surprisingly, considering to whom he was speaking, focused in particular on the vow of celibacy. He told us that celibacy was much more than physical virginity, and that abstaining from physical sexual activity while allowing oneself to become cold, hard and self-centred was not living the vow in the way it was intended. 'I would even suggest,' he said, 'that allowing oneself to become that sort of person is probably a bigger sin than fornication – not that I am recommending either, of course.' He went on to tell us about the freedom that a celibate life well-lived can give to a person, freedom to love humanity generally rather than one person in particular. Celibacy, he said, was in the service of ministry to the people.

Listening to him I recognised this as the message I had been hearing from preachers and teachers since my earliest years. But now it raised more questions than it answered. I knew that there was truth in what he was saying, but only some. Was celibacy really in the service of ministry to people, or was it in the service of an institutional church? So much has changed since I first heard the message forty years ago. Now we live in a dramatically different world, with sexual attitudes varying from the modesty of the Islamic women covered over by their burkahs to the blatant pornography of many television channels, and certain sites on the internet. The church's theology of sexuality has also changed dramatically in those forty years, from a negative and highly restrictive attitude to one that proclaims the beauty of sexual relationships in marriage. We have had to come to terms with a high level of sexual deviation among priests and religious, and in particular the harrowing problem of child sexual abuse by ministers of the church. There is little or no doubt that the dramatic decline in vocations in the western world is to some extent due to

the law of compulsory celibacy for priests. In this context, a new
and more searching examination of celibacy is in urgent need of
taking place. The old answers are no longer good enough.

The Problem of the Church and Homosexuality

In my work as a travelling preacher I am very impressed by many
of the priests I meet. Another man I worked with recently, again
serving a parish on his own, and no longer in the flush of youth,
was extraordinarily committed and effective. He told me how he
was very involved in the sporting life of the parish, even in training the local senior team. In this way he had a unique and price-
less contact with the young men and women of the area, the age-
group that are not seen very much in church any more. 'They
might not come to mass every Sunday,' he said, 'but I see them
regularly enough. They go to communion when they are there,
and I wouldn't dream of making a fuss about that, even if they
have missed mass the previous few Sundays. I'm just glad to see
them in the church, and I make a point of being welcoming towards them.' I complimented him. I could see from the statistics
of his parish, and the high rate of mass attendance, that he was
doing well. I particularly remarked on his energy and enthusiasm,
at this stage in his life, to be so involved in the sporting life of the
parish. 'I meet very few like you any more,' I said. 'Twenty years
ago many priests were involved at that level, but not now. This is
particularly true of the small number of young priests we have.
Most of them seem to have no interest in sport'. His response
brought up an issue that concerns many people in the church
today, but which it is difficult to speak or write openly about.
'Most of them are gay,' he said.

   The question of homosexuality and homosexual relationships
is becoming a major issue both in church and society. Commentators reckon that the fear that gay marriage might be given legal
recognition was one of the factors that influenced people in America

to vote for George Bush in the last election. Some months ago a lesbian couple, who were married in Canada, brought the issue to the forefront of life here by pursuing a case through the Irish courts for the recognition of their union, with the privileges and tax concessions that go with it. Irish politicians who have spoken on the issue seem to be adopting a position that gay relationships deserve recognition, but that classifying them as marriages is a bridge too far for the Irish voter.

In my work as a priest I do not find it easy to uphold the church's teaching on homosexuality. My experience of homosexuals, particularly men, would suggest that many of them have a deep spiritual life, and long to give this communal expression. They have told me about their desire to belong to the Catholic church, but they feel condemned and rejected by us. When the church describes their orientation as an 'objective disorder', and condemns all homosexual acts as 'intrinsically evil', or 'acts of grave depravity' it is hard to expect them to feel kindly towards the church, or to be at home there. I honestly do not think it is either fair or realistic to expect all people of a homosexual orientation to remain celibate throughout their lives, and to refrain from any form of physical sexual expression. When this is made a condition of their belonging to the church it is no wonder that so many walk away sadly. In the last number of years the church has taken an increasingly hard line on this. A good illustration is the case of Sr Jeanine Gramick and Fr Bob Nugent, an American nun and priest who worked for many years with the homosexual community, but who were forbidden to continue by the Vatican authorities in 1999 because they were not willing to give total external and internal adherence to the church's teaching. I imagine that many priests and religious, if we were put through a similar rigorous interrogation, would equally fail the test. The text of the correspondence between them and the Vatican, which is available on the internet, makes for fascinating reading. For instance, in arguing against Gramick and Nugent where they appeal to the message of love preached by Jesus, the Vatican document says the following: 'Here the serious errors of the authors' positions become especially clear, as there is, and in fact can be, no opposition between Jesus' message of love and the teaching of the church'. I wish that were true. Even a cursory reading of church history points to many illustrations of church teaching being very opposed to Jesus' message of love.

And yet, paradoxically, the Catholic priesthood seems to be a profession chosen by an increasing number of gay men. Statistics on this are hard, indeed impossible, to get. The American writer, Donald B. Cozzens, a former rector of a seminary, claimed in his book *The Changing Face of the Priesthood* that some seminaries in the United States had a gay population as high as 75 per cent. Around the same time an American newspaper, the *Kansas City Star*, suggested that the proportionate AIDS death rate among Catholic priests in the States was at least four times that of the general population. It must be stated that I am not aware of any scientific basis for either of these statements.

What is the situation in the priesthood in Ireland? There are even fewer statistics available here. But I believe there is a perception that our seminaries (the few that are left) have a substantial number of students of homosexual orientation. It is impossible to be sure. One student explained to me recently how students for the priesthood will do their best to hide their orientation for fear of expulsion. I understand that some of the religious orders are more open to accepting homosexuals who acknowledge their orientation than the national seminary. As I travel the country on mission work many priests of my age-group, like the man I describe above, raise with me their concern that a great many of the younger priests seem to be homosexual.

I am aware that in writing this I could be accused of being homophobic. I hope I am not. Since all priests take a vow of celibacy, and are presumed to live their lives without any physical sexual expression, should it make any difference what orientation they are? At one level it doesn't, and I know that homosexual men are as entitled and as suited to be priests as anyone else.

It is difficult to talk or write about it because the whole issue of sexual orientation is hedged around with so many prejudices. Even those of us who might believe we are free of prejudice can still be labouring under deep unconscious biases. But if the percentage of gays in the priesthood is far higher than the population average, as is the general perception, then I do believe we have a situation that needs to be looked at. That is why it needs to be raised as an issue in a book like this. Is it the enclosed, male, clerical system that I have written about in an earlier chapter of this book that attracts gay men to the priesthood? Is it compulsory celibacy that is discouraging heterosexual men from becoming priests? These are large and difficult questions, but they absolutely need to be faced. If we do not face them honestly we will run the risk of allowing ministerial priesthood in the Catholic church to become the domain of one small section of society, gay men. If the priesthood consists of a majority of gay men it will, I believe, be further evidence of a dysfunctional church.

The Growth of Fundamentalism

When I began my life as a priest thirty years ago I believed that we were heading into a time when reason and reflection would shape religious belief and practice. I felt that the age of narrow judgemental attitudes that led to bitterness and war between religions was over. But instead we have lived to see religious expression dominated by fundamentalism, an authoritarian, black and white view of what is to be believed. This is characterised by a literal interpretation of the Bible, or in the case of Islam, the Koran. Fundamentalists have a conviction of the rightness of their own beliefs, and that everyone else is wrong. Their way is the only way. Often enough it goes farther than that. Some believers today are convinced that they, and what they believe, represent the good, and that all opposing beliefs are evil, and the work of Satan. It seems to be the belief of George Bush, on the one hand, and Osama bin Laden on the other. Both tend to use the same type of language and imagery. We are good; our opponents are evil. In fact, the really striking thing is the similarity between fundamentalist views irrespective of where they originate from, and despite the fact that those who hold them often hate and despise each other.

Fundamentalism is the fastest growing form of religious belief today. Maybe it is a retreat from the complexity of life, a search for simple and secure answers. It is almost as if we have reverted back to the era of the great religious wars of the sixteenth and seventeenth centuries. There is an increase in hatred and bitterness, the type of attitudes that led to those wars, and could well lead to a much more destructive conflagration between Christianity and Islam. It is hard to see how attitudes which create so much division and hatred can be expressions of religious belief. But in a world of sudden and dramatic change, maybe it is not surprising that people are drawn to the type of easy certainties that fundamentalist beliefs seem to provide.

In the past the Catholic church has at times flirted with fundamentalist attitudes. Up until recently it believed that it had the whole truth, and that anyone outside the Catholic fold was in error. It even went so far at times as to attempt to condemn them all to eternal damnation. Thankfully, no religious group can abrogate the authority of God over the salvation of humanity. Today, the Catholic church has a new role. It needs to provide a bastion, a voice of reason and openness, against the rise of fundamentalism. Of all world religions it is best qualified for this role, and to some extent it is doing so. Despite all its faults and failings of the past, the church has an unrivalled intellectual tradition, a tradition of rigorous philosophical and theological study. This has been one of its more attractive qualities and has saved it from descending into sentimentality and piety. It is also a world-wide organisation that supersedes all cultures and nationally or regionally-based beliefs. But there are forces within the church that are attracted to the beliefs and attitudes of the fundamentalist. They look at the success of the evangelical groups, particularly in the Americas and Africa, and they are tempted to say that it is the way to go. This would be a dreadful mistake for the church given that reason and reflection, study and understanding, have been a significant part of our tradition. Now, more than ever before, we need to emphasise these features, even if at the moment they seem not to be successful in terms of attracting people. After all, our founder ended his life with only a small handful of followers. The size of the crowd is never a good indication of the truth.

Pope John Paul II
Now that Pope John Paul is dead, and we have distanced ourselves a little from the extraordinary events surrounding his final illness, death and funeral, it may be possible to begin to make some assessment of his contribution to the church and the world.

In September 1979, after one year in office, Pope John Paul II came on a visit to Ireland. It was an extraordinary occasion, when the whole country came to a standstill for three days, and enormous crowds gathered wherever he went. As a young priest I attended the famous youth gathering at the racecourse in Galway. Most people who were there still remember the atmosphere and the singing and cheering. To see a pope being greeted in Ireland like a pop star was amazing. We got the first illustration of something we became very familiar with over the years of his papacy, this pope's ability to work and respond to a crowd. He was, and continued to be even in extreme old age and disability, a man of extraordinary charisma. I was up on the stage, concelebrating the mass. When it was over I happened to be beside the passageway along which the pope would pass on his way down. I was going to be in a perfect position to shake his hand. But as he came close I was conscious of an older priest straining from behind me to reach out and touch the pope. I stood back and let him in to my position. I knew he would appreciate the honour much more than me. Despite all the euphoria, I left the gathering that day with a sense of foreboding. It was already obvious that we had as our pope a man of considerable substance, but some of whose attitudes and actions gave cause for concern.

Pope John Paul II has moved upon the world stage for the past quarter century with great distinction. It would probably be fair to say that he has been the most influential and impressive figure of the last part of the twentieth century. He undoubtedly was influential in the collapse of the communist system in Eastern Europe through his assault on the regime in his native Poland. History will certainly give him credit as a major player in those events, though it is probably true that the Soviet Union was by then collapsing in on itself in any case. He was the great moral and religious leader of his time, travelling the world with undying energy to spread the message of the Christian faith. As Catholics, we had many reasons to be proud of our pope.

He was most outstandingly a man of peace. Even though he had much in common with George Bush he did not support the war in Iraq, but took a firm and consistent line against it. His final visit to Lourdes in August 2004, when he knelt at the grotto and prayed for peace, is an inspiring image:

Join me in imploring the Virgin Mary to obtain for our world the longed-for gift of peace. May forgiveness and brotherly love take root in human hearts. May every weapon by laid down and all hatred and violence put aside. May everyone see in his neighbour not an enemy to be fought, but a brother to be accepted and loved, so that we may join in building a better world.

This was Pope John Paul II at his best, exercising his role as the great religious leader and enunciating the longings of the human heart. Here he was not just a pope for the Catholics. He spoke for everyone. He was truly a world figure.

Pope John Paul's papacy was not all positive. When it comes to assessing his government of the Catholic church the judgement is mixed. He was elected pope fourteen years after the Vatican Council had ended. Those years had been difficult ones for the church. The council had created great expectations, but it had not brought about the structural changes necessary (e.g. reform of the Curia) for the fulfilment of these expectations. That all remained to be done. Those fourteen years were characterised by a struggle between those who wanted to pursue the agenda of change and those who wanted to halt it and keep things as they had been. Pope Paul VI was a good man, but not decisive by nature, and as the years passed and his health deteriorated, he was less able to give leadership. *Humanae Vitae* was so controversial that it served to blight his reign. So Pope John Paul II took over a church that was engaged in intense debate over many issues to do with church government and moral teaching. Unlike Paul VI he had the personal strength of character and moral stature to give good leadership. Unfortunately he positioned himself at one extreme side of the debate. He had the capacity to be a unifying force in the church, being available to both sides and helping to bring them together. Instead, by adopting one extreme position in a dogmatic and authoritarian way, he alienated the other side. As a consequence his years as pope were characterised by division and bitterness within the church. At the end of his reign, the church was more polarised than at any time since the council. Unfortunately, the divisions increasingly focused on the person of the pope himself. By lining himself up with the most conservative and traditional factions within the church he has made them his great defenders. Orthodoxy was increasingly assessed not on a person's commitment to Christ and his teaching, but rather on his loyalty to the pope.

The other disappointing feature of the reign of Pope John Paul II was his failure to promote the agenda of the Vatican Council. This was particularly evident in relation to the governance of the church. The council clearly wished for a greater involvement of the bishops in church leadership, and a lessening of the influence of the Curia. In Pope John Paul's time the opposite happened. What was meant to be a council of bishops directly involved in the running of the church was reduced to a synod of bishops which was little more than a talking shop and which didn't even have the authority to write its own report. Simultaneously the Curia became more powerful than it had been for many years. At the end of Pope John Paul's papacy the church was more centralised than at any time since the death of Pope Pius XII. In this very important area he has guided the church in the opposite way to what the council intended and wished.

An inevitable result of centralised government is the weakening of leadership in the regions. We have certainly seen that in the church. With Rome so active, dogmatic and authoritarian, individual bishops became more cautious about their own decision-making. They constantly looked over their shoulders to see what Rome was saying, and focused more often on keeping in with Rome than on making the best decision for the particular situation in their diocese. Pope John Paul II's policy of appointing bishops was also problematic. As I've said elsewhere, he pursued a policy of making appointments to bishoprics based on the person's perceived orthodoxy rather than their ability. The effect of these two developments has been serious for the church particularly when it came to the issue of clerical child sexual abuse.

Bishops, who had operated with little real authority and with a policy of appeasement of Rome, now found themselves incapable of acting decisively. Consequently we witnessed the inadequacy of the response of the church, which has proved to be probably a bigger scandal than the abuse itself. In his role as pontiff Pope John Paul II was slow to admit the gravity of the situation. There has to be a suspicion that he put the good name of the church before the value of the individual. It is ironic that this should happen to someone who in other areas of life was a resounding defender of the dignity of every human person. It is an example of what can happen to a person when they get caught up in the structure of an institution.

Pope John Paul II was a man of great contradictions. In his early years he travelled the world, particularly to places like Poland and South America, and spoke wonderfully to massive gatherings about the dignity of the human person and the central importance of freedom. He attacked dogmatic and authoritarian regimes for the way they oppressed their people. Internally, within the church in these same countries, in meetings with bishops and priests, it was a different matter. He told them they must be obedient to the magisterium of the church (meaning the Vatican), and he criticised any sign of independent thinking or action among them. We all remember his finger wagging at the priest who was a government minister in El Salvador. The message was clear. It was all right to be political in Poland but not in South America.

On moral issues he was inflexible. While it is important that the church has clear moral positions on the various issues of the day, this should always be tempered by compassion. It appeared as if people's membership of the church was dependent on living by specific moral standards rather than by virtue of their baptism. The church has traditionally tried to preserve a balance between its moral teaching and its pastoral practice. While upholding the teaching, it has encouraged flexibility in practice, to allow for the weakness of human nature. During the papacy of Pope John Paul II this important balance was upset. Moral standards imposed without understanding and compassion can prove impossible for people in particular situations in life. For those people the church appeared harsh and judgemental, and they felt excluded. Ultimately, the church must be more concerned with preaching the compassion of Jesus rather than laying down the law.

In the debate that has gone on since his death the issues I have raised above have been mentioned by many. I found myself very much in agreement with one commentator who said that she liked him more as he got older. She believed that in his later years he had mellowed, lost his earlier hectoring style, and became a better listener. The witness he gave during his last months of sickness was impressive. The sight of this old man, clearly in pain and suffering, but still continuing to put his dedication to duty ahead of personal comfort, was a powerful message to the world. Some commentators suggested that this period of his life was the most fruitful, that it was his great period of witness to Christ, the suffering Christ.

The events surrounding the death and funeral of Pope John Paul II were extraordinary by any standards. It was almost the only story on all the major media outlets for nearly a week. The crowds that gathered in Rome were enormous, and there was no doubt that many people were deeply bereaved by his death. There was a genuine and heartfelt outbreak of emotion right across the world. The two groups of people who were most notably present and affected were Poles and young people. For Poles he was a national hero, who had brought them their freedom. It was easy to see why they loved him. His attraction to young people isn't quite so easy to explain. Some say it is because he was a clear and decisive moral teacher, along with being a type of father figure. I'm sure there is some truth to that. But it seems to me that many

young people were attracted to him without having much commitment to what he stood for, or wishing to follow the moral
guidance that he was giving them. There was an element of the
media star about him that drew them. The comment of a young
Italian girl who had attended one of the world youth events was
interesting. 'It was like attending a rock concert that our parents
approved of,' she said. I know that there were some young people
who were deeply impressed by him, and who have formed themselves into various youth organisations that are committed to
everything he stood for. But these seem to me to be a very small
minority of those who admired him. Only time will tell what his
real impact on today's young generation was. Many in the church
in Ireland believed after the big youth mass in Galway in 1979,
and the euphoric greeting given to him by the young people of
Ireland, that it would signal a turning back to the church by the
youth. We know that did not happen.

One of the very interesting aspects of the whole event was the
response of the media. From the few days before his death to the
conclusion of the funeral they largely lost their critical faculty.
They were absorbed and impressed by all the ritual and pageantry surrounding the occasion. I know that so much of it was beautiful, but it also contained elements that were redolent of times
long gone. Women were almost invisible at the funeral, apart from
one reader and a few in the offertory procession. Even the choir
was all male. And yet that was hardly commented on. I know that
it was a time to be positive, and to enter into the drama and emotion of the event. But I was surprised to see apparently hard-head-
ed media people being so carried away by something of which
they would normally disapprove. Maybe it is an indication of how
starved the modern world is of ritual and pageantry. They also
loved the Conclave, and all the ancient ritual around that. Very
few commented on the extraordinary anomaly of a small group of
very old men choosing a leader for the Catholic world. Does all

this mean that from now on the media will be much more positively disposed to the Catholic church? I doubt it, but only time will tell.

For me the whole event, from the funeral to the election of the new pope, while beautiful in many ways, was also illustrative of many of the things that I believe are wrong with the church at the moment, and which I have dealt with in this book.

The Legacy of Pope John Paul II

What will be the legacy of Pope John Paul II? And what will be his long-term influence on the church? John Cornwell, in his book *The Pope in Winter*, has this to say:

> Throughout the worldwide church one finds everywhere vibrant Catholic communities; people working, and dying, for the faith; selfless ministers, sisters and laity working for the sick and the poor; members of the faithful making the world a better place. The spirit of Vatican II is at work and cannot be quenched. But there are countless millions of Catholics who have fallen away because they have become demoralised and excluded under John Paul II. His major and abiding legacy, I believe, is to be seen and felt in various forms of oppression, and exclusion, trust in papal absolutism and antagonistic divisions. Never have Catholics been so divided, never has there been so much contempt and aggression between Catholics. Never has the local church suffered so much at the hands of the Vatican and the papal centre.

That is a fairly harsh assessment of Pope John Paul II, written shortly before he died, and one that I feel is not fully justified. There is so much that was good about him that balanced out and possibly outweighed his failures. The genuine sense of loss that was felt when he died is an indication of that, though, as I have said above, it is too soon to draw any definite conclusions. But there is no doubt that his successor, Benedict XVI, will have a difficult task, made more so I believe by some of the policies pursued under the papacy of his predecessor. If Pope Benedict surprises us, as some predict he will, and pursues a more progressive line, being willing to listen and consult, and implementing the decisions of the Vatican Council, he will be vehemently opposed by the more traditional groups that had immense power under Pope John Paul. Organisations like Opus Dei and the Legionaries of Christ do not appear to be interested in compromise. They seem to be convinced of the rightness of their point of view. If the church tries to move in a way that is different to what they stand for there is real possibility of a split. It was a big mistake to give them the type of power and distinction that Pope John Paul II gave them.

If on the other hand Pope Benedict adopts the same policies as his predecessor I don't anticipate a split in the church. Instead there will inevitably be an even larger falling away from membership of those who have hung on in the hope of change. Earlier statements by Cardinal Ratzinger would indicate that he is very critical of western society, particularly what he sees as its self-centredness and its relativism. I hope he does not continue to pursue this line as pope. I believe it is crucial that the church enter into dialogue with life as it is lived in the west. If it continues to adopt an attitude of condemnation, while attempting to impose rigid moral positions, it will simply alienate more people. Some say that it does not really matter, because the future of the church is in the southern hemisphere, especially Africa and South America. This makes no sense to me, because as these countries get more prosperous they will inevitably take on many of the attitudes of the west. We are seeing it happening now in Eastern Europe. If the church is not able to communicate to developed societies it will be failing in its duty to preach the Gospel. It is important that the spirituality and the challenging social message of Christianity be preserved in the developed world.

The other big task facing the new pope in my opinion is to become a focus for unity within the church as well as outside. What I mean is that he tries to create conversation between the different views and groups in the church. I agree with what John L. Allen recently said in his weekly 'Letter from Rome':

> Today spiritual offerings are increasingly tailored to the con-sumer preference of niche groups. Liturgical traditionalists, charismatics, peace-and-justice activists and liberal reformers all have their own publications, conferences, even movements and parishes in most dioceses. Catholics who move in one circle can sometimes go through life never interacting with someone from another. In light of the ecclesiology of communion, this is problematic. All sectors of life in the church, including those in the social apostolate, will have to strive to carve out spaces where conversation can happen.

Can Pope Benedict achieve this? I don't know. Despite the disappointment of many people at his election, our hope has to be that he will govern in a way that is most beneficial for the church in this time.

X

CHANGES THAT COULD HAPPEN QUICKLY

In writing this book I am acutely aware that it is much easier to diagnose what is wrong than to make suggestions as to how it can be put right. It is hard for any of us to prescribe a new way of doing things. It is also true that change is usually not planned, but occurs in response to new and often unforeseen demands or situations. I have proposed some substantial changes for the church in this book, but one of the great lessons from the history of the church is that change does not come easily or quickly. Maybe some of my proposals are unrealistic. It is not likely that I will see a major reform of the Vatican structure or of church ministry in my lifetime. But it is important to keep the vision of a different way of doing things before us.

In an effort to apply theory to practice, as I end this book, I will make three suggestions that I think we could begin to move towards immediately. Indeed work on them is already in progress in some places.

On the Side of the Poor

When John the Baptist was in prison and was beginning to have doubts about Jesus, he sent a messenger to him to know if he was the one that was expected. The answer Jesus gave is very revealing. It tells us what he considered to be the core and defining mark of his teaching:

> Go and tell John what you have heard and seen. The blind see, the lame walk, lepers are cleansed, the deaf hear, the dead are raised to life and the poor have the Good News preached to them.

Clearly the big test of the Christian, either as individual or as community, is how we respond to the poor. In Ireland we have focused a lot of our energy in the past on getting people to practise their religion, meaning attendance at mass and the sacraments. That has its own importance. Coming together as a community of believers to express and celebrate our faith is an essential part of being a church. But it wasn't the acid test laid down by Jesus. As a Catholic community we must be on the side of the poor, the marginalised, those whom society rejects. Every local community of Christian believers must have an outreach to those in need. In other words, people who are poor, a person in despair or suicidal, a young pregnant girl, a husband and wife whose marriage is in difficulty, the aids sufferer or any person in need, would know that within the Catholic community they would find acceptance, understanding and help. That would mean creating structures, some of which are already in place. We have organisations like Cura, St Vincent de Paul and others who are doing some of this. But we need many more, and ones that are more localised, more identified with the local community of believers. About forty years ago in this country there was a move to set up social services in some dioceses and a few had very successful social service organisations which were visible signs of the church's care for the poor. Unfortunately, as time went by these services came to rely on state funding and consequently lost their independence, being eventually largely subsumed into the state model. We need to revisit these initiatives. We could have a social service organisation in each diocese that would be funded by the diocese, locally based in the communities, and with services available to anybody in need. This would need to be owned and supported by the people, so that they would be willing to contribute what is necessary to fund it. The Catholic community would have to undergo a mind shift which accepts that contributing to such a service is as integral a part of our religion as mass attendance. The present custom of throwing a coin into the basket at weekend mass would have to be replaced by the contribution of a substantial donation that would be a sign of real commitment. It is one of the particular problems of the Irish church. The small contributions made by the believers were enough to support a poorly paid clergy in the past, but will be utterly inadequate to pay full-time lay workers, not to mention the sort of initiative I am suggesting here. Being funded by the church and independent of the state system would give this type of social service much greater flexibility and availability. Some paid staff would need to be employed who would advocate on behalf of the people who are in need. Such an initiative would be a real witness to the fact that the Christian community recognised that service to the poor is an essential part of Christian living and not an optional extra.

An Inclusive Church
The second area where I feel we could make real headway in a short space of time is in creating a church that is inclusive. By that I mean a church that is open to everyone who wishes to be a member. One of the outstanding features of the ministry of Jesus, and one that made many enemies for him, was his acceptance of everybody, be they sinners, outcasts, lepers, whatever. On the other hand the real signal that a church has developed into a sect is when they begin to exclude people, when they begin to divide the world into those who are chosen and those who are not. An inclusive church would need to send out a clear message that everyone is welcome. Nobody should be excluded, no matter what state their lives are in, or what their orientation may be. In fact, the person whose life is in a mess, or who is clearly not succeeding in living the Christian ideal, should be particularly welcome. Of course, if a person is hardened in a destructive or sinful way of life they will not want to be part of the community. The only requirement necessary for membership should be that the person

wants to belong. This will demand great openness and tolerance from the members, and an end to judgemental attitudes. One of the big temptations of religious people is to become judgemental, to begin to see themselves as better than others, and to look down in condemnation on those who appear not to be living by the same high standards as themselves. Where this occurs it is a particularly unpleasant side-effect of religious belief. It seems to have been especially prevalent in the time of Jesus. I know that some people will see the type of open community I am describing as a watering down of Christian moral values. They will point to the words Jesus spoke to the woman caught in adultery: 'Go in peace, but do not sin again'. Jesus did not use that sentence as a threat. He was not telling her that if she continued to sin she would have no business coming back to him. What he meant was that her sinful life was destructive of herself and others, and that she would only find peace when she changed and began to live by different values. That is the ideal for all Christian communities. They would not impose their values by excluding people, but rather by encouragement and good example. Sinners recognised the futility and hopelessness of their lifestyle when they came face to face with the goodness of Jesus, and they wanted to change. The same dynamic should work within the Christian community. So let's not exclude anyone. Make them welcome, and give them motivation and support in their efforts to become new and better people.

This development in pastoral practice will not come from the Vatican. The authorities there will continue to tell us that, among others, people in second relationships after their first marriage has broken up, or gay people in a sexual union, are in a state of serious sin, and cannot receive the sacraments unless they promise to give up their behaviour. We must not wait for a lead from the Vatican on this one. The bishops could act on it. I have argued that the church needs to be decentralised and that the pope should be 'first among equals', not superior to his brother bishops.

Traditionally a bishop in his own diocese had much more power and autonomy than is being exercised at present. If the bishops of a country, for instance Ireland, proclaimed that all Christian communities must be inclusive and that no person should be refused the sacraments, there would be little or nothing that the Vatican could do about it. A unified body of bishops making a statement like that would be a wonderful message of compassion from the church. If all the Irish bishops could not agree on this message of inclusivity then maybe a number of them together could do so. If the bishops could not find their way to do this, maybe some priests, together with the pastoral council of the parish, could issue an invitation to all people to come to the table of the Eucharist, not as a concession but as a right.

Involvement of People
The third commitment that the church could make immediately is to include lay people as fully as possible in the sacramental life of the church. Already much is happening in this area, but it is uneven both in terms of policy and action. If all dioceses were to make it a corner-stone of their approach at all levels it would send out a strong message. Appointments of priests to parishes would be clearly understood as implying a willingness to work in collaboration with the local people. As the shortage of priests creates vacancies, and priests are brought in from other countries, this would be one of the conditions under which they would come. A priest coming into a parish and disbanding the existing structures of lay involvement would no longer be tolerated. As a specific expression of this, each parish could be instructed to have a liturgy group that would be actively involved in the organisation and preparation of all Sunday masses and other liturgical events.

I think that these three suggestions are all possible, and that they would make a great difference to the church at local level, which of course is where church is really church.

I live in hope. Every Christian must do that. Hope is of the essence of our faith. No matter what problems we face, the Spirit of God is with us. God can bring good out of every situation, and his Spirit can work wonders in the most infertile ground, can bring life out of the most hopeless situations. I draw great comfort and strength from the Prophet Isaiah:

> Let the wilderness and dry lands exult,
> Let the wasteland rejoice and bloom,
> Let it bring forth flowers like the jonquil,
> Let it rejoice and sing for joy.

Looking at the church today we see plenty of signs of wilderness and dry lands. To many observers it seems like a wasteland. But in the Christian understanding of reality the wasteland is precisely where the new life is most likely to flourish, and there are signs of new life. There are young lay catechists who are trying to pass on the Christian message to our second-level students and who are working enthusiastically in the face of indifference from some students and parents. There are lay people quietly running their own prayer groups, meditation groups without any assistance from the clerical church. There are church communities that are reaching out to those in great need. Many church communities are welcoming our new immigrants. There are priests who have great skill in, and commitment to, the involvement of lay people in ministry. My final plea is that we not give way to dejection but concentrate on the edict of Isaiah:

> Strengthen all weary hands
> Steady all trembling knees
> And say to all faint hearts
> Courage! Do not be afraid.

FURTHER READING

This is a list of books for those who would like to read further on any of the issues that are raised in this book.

HARING, BERNARD. He was undoubtedly the outstanding moral theologian of the twentieth century in the Catholic church. His two major works were *The Law of Christ* and *Free and Faithful in Christ*. He spent most of his life lecturing in a seminary in Rome. When he retired he moved back to his native Germany where he battled with sickness until he died in his eighties. *My Hope for the Church* (Redemptorist Publications, 1999) was written shortly before he died. It is his final statement on the church that he loved all his life. It is readable and challenging. Highly recommended.

KUNG, HANS. Professor Kung has had an uneasy relationship with the church, especially during the reign of Pope John Paul II. But he still remains a committed Catholic and priest. He played a significant part in the Second Vatican Council as a young theologian and has written extensively ever since. His books are all worth reading and are generally quite accessible even for the person with no theological background. Some people say that his best book is *On Being a Christian*. I would recommend the following:

Christianity, the Religious Situation of Our Time (SCM Press, 1995); *A History of the Church* (invaluable in giving the background to many of the questions and difficulties facing the church today); *My Struggle for Freedom* (Continuum, 2003) – the first volume of his memoirs. He is working on the second volume. It is interesting for the general reader in giving the inside story of the Second Vatican Council, the debates and power struggles that took place, and Kung's assessment of its successes and failures. For those who are particularly interested in the issue of papal infallibility, Kung has a little book: *Infallible?* (William Collins, 1971).

DUFFY, EAMON. *Saints and Sinners, A History of the Popes* (Yale University Press, 1997) – a marvellous account of the history of the papacy, from its beginning up to the reign of Pope John Paul II.

BROWN, RAYMOND E. Brown is the colossus of Scripture scholars of our time. In relation to the issues covered in my book I would recommend the following titles:

The Birth of the Messiah (Geoffrey Chapman, 1977). The classic text on the birth of Jesus as told in the Gospels. But it is academic and does not make for easy reading.

The Churches the Apostles left Behind (Paulist Press, 1984). This deals with the early Christian communities and how the church developed.

Biblical Reflections on Crises Facing the Church (Paulist Press, 1975). Covers such issues as the ordination of women, the papacy, the role of Mary and ecumenism.

Even though it is now thirty years or so since Brown was writing his main works, he is still the greatest authority in Catholic Biblical scholarship.

RICHARDS, HUBERT J. *The First Christmas, What Really Happened?* (Collins. 1973). An excellent little book, giving a simple and easily read account of Biblical scholarship on the stories told about the birth of Jesus. For those who might find Raymond Brown too difficult, Richards gives much the same material in a simpler fashion.

Another book on the same topic is *The Infancy Narratives* by Herman Hendrickx (Geoffrey Chapman, 1984).

WEST, MORRIS. Morris West is an Australian novelist, born in 1916. His best known works are *The Devil's Advocate* and *The Shoes of the Fisherman*. In his early life he spent ten years as a member of the Christian Brothers. *A View from the Ridge* (Harper Collins, 1996) was written when he was eighty years of age. It gives an account of his religious development and his current assessment of the Catholic church. It is a wonderful little book.

SCHILLEBEECKX, EDWARD. *The Church with a Human Face, A New and Expanded Theology of Ministry* (SCM Press, 1985). Schillebeeckx is not the easiest to read, but for those who are willing to make the effort this book gives a good understanding of the whole issue of ministry in the church, its origins and where we might go from here.

MOREA, PETER C. *Towards a Liberal Catholicism, Psychology and Four Women* (SCM Press, 2000). An interesting book on the church. The title makes the stance of the author clear. He argues his position very convincingly.

BAIGENT, MICHAEL and LEIGH, RICHARD. *The Inquisition* (Penguin Books, 1999). These writers are better known for *Holy Blood, Holy Grail*, which was probably the inspiration behind *The Da Vinci Code*. Their book on the Inquisition, one of the most inglorious eras in the history of the church, is better researched and more interesting.

WILLS, GARRY. *Papal Sins* (Darton, Longman and Todd, 2000). A bestseller in America when first published. It is a very readable and fascinating account of the papacy.

QUINN, JOHN R. *The Reform of the Papacy* (Crossroad Herder & Herder, 1999).

SIPE, RICHARD. *Sex, Priests and Power, Anatomy of a Crisis* (Cassell, 1995). Richard Sipe is one of the more thought-provoking Catholic writers on sexuality and the church's sexual teaching.

KELLY, KEVIN T. *Divorce and Second Marriage, Facing the Challenge* (Collins, 1982). Kevin Kelly is a well-known writer on moral theology, and is a parish priest in Cheshire, England. He has written many books and articles and is a regular contributor to *The Furrow*. Well worth reading.

LAWLER, MICHAEL G. *Secular Marriage, Christian Sacrament* (Twenty-Third Publications, 1985). The whole area of marriage, divorce and annulment is a tortuous one for the church, and I have only briefly referred to it in this book. There is a great deal written on the subject. This book is just one of many.

FAGAN, S.M., SEAN. *Does Morality Change?* (Gill and Macmillan 1997). One of the better books to come out of the Irish theological scene in recent times. It was recently censured by either the Vatican or the Irish bishops – it was hard to be sure where the censure came from as it was published on the Internet!

    Quench not the Spirit (Columba, 2005) is a collection of essays recently published in honour of Sean Fagan.

LAKELAND, PAUL. *The Liberation of the Laity, In Search of an Accountable Church* (Continuum, 2002). There are many books being written on the role of the laity in the church at present. This book surveys both historical and contemporary writing on the subject, and then goes on to suggest where we can go from here.

WIJNGAARDS, JOHN. *The Ordination of Women in the Catholic Church, Unmasking a Cuckoo's Egg Tradition* (Media House, 2002). Wijngaards is an acknowledged expert on the subject of the ordination of women.

BYRNE, LAVINIA. *Woman at the Altar, the Ordination of Women in the Roman Catholic Church* (Mobray, 1994 & 1998). Lavinia Byrne came under the censure of the Vatican a few years ago for her views on this matter.

CORNWELL, JOHN. *The Pope in Winter, the Dark Face of John Paul II's Papacy* (Penguin, 2005). One of many books on Pope John Paul II. It is written from a fairly critical point of view, but it also gives a great picture of the man and what motivated him.

DOSTOEVSKY, FYODOR. *The Brothers Karamazov* (Vintage, 1992) – One of the classics of Russian literature. Particularly recommended is the chapter on The Grand Inquisitor.